Get Your Head in the Cloud
Unraveling the Mystery for Public Sector

© 2012 GTSI Press, by Jim Sweeney

ISBN 978-1-105-64720-8

Dedication

This book is dedicated to Sterling Phillips, CEO of GTSI. Without his vision and belief in my talents, this book would not have been possible.

A little over a year ago, in the spring of 2011, Sterling was nominated to serve on the TechAmerica Cloud2 Commission, initiated by Vivek Kundra, federal government CIO. The purpose of the Cloud2 Commission was to generate a report containing recommendations on how the federal government could take better advantage of Cloud technology.

After Sterling agreed to serve on the commission, he called me. I was in Orlando speaking on virtualization and Cloud to the statewide conference of IT professionals. On our call, Sterling warmly explained to me that, while he was a commissioner (along with 70 other leaders from industry), the way these things usually worked was that there were a lot of industry heavyweights, but accompanying each of them was a "big-brained person" to act as their deputy and frankly "do 99% of the work." He then proceeded to ask me if I would be his "big-brained person," otherwise known as his deputy, for the TechAmerica Cloud2 Commission.

At the time, I was so flabbergasted that I mumbled something in reply to his invitation like, "Happy to do it, but I think all the big-brained folks at GTSI are busy!"

Serving on the commission as Sterling's deputy has provided me with incredible insight into the challenges – and rewards – of incorporating Cloud technology into the public sector. Sterling, I cannot thank you enough for giving me this opportunity!

Acknowledgements

I've heard it said
That people come into our lives for a reason
Bringing something we must learn
And we are led
To those who help us most to grow
If we let them
And we help them in return.

From the musical "Wicked"

I'd like to acknowledge the following individuals for their invaluable guidance and assistance in making this book possible:

Sterling Phillips, CEO of GTSI Corp., for offering me the opportunity to write this book.

Chris Gorski, for his in-depth knowledge of the PaaS environment and contributions to the PaaS chapter.

Don Upson, for his invaluable insights and tireless efforts to promote the book even before it was written.

Former Congressman *Tom Davis* for the foreward to the book.

The behind-the-scenes staff that helped put this book together: Gerson Arias, Amey Bartholow, designers; Tina Payne, staff; and Sue Williams, editor.

The reviewers both internal and external to GTSI, including Rich Anton, Gerson Arias, Whit Crump, Brett Roth, and Miguel Sian for all their time and effort to help make this a great product.

And finally, all my friends and family including the Saturday night card club, Bill, DJ, Gary, Jim and Joan, Josh and Dana, Len, MK, Nick, Ryan, Sue, and of course, Jon.

Foreward

Cloud computing is a game changer, a technology tsunami. It washes over and away practically every serious notion most of us have ever held about how we own, maintain, secure and manage our IT infrastructure.

Equally powerful, the Cloud changes the way we access, store, utilize and pay for data and applications – our own and others.

It is revolutionary, dramatic and societal in its impact. Cloud computing is a technology epoch, just as introduction of the PC was in the late 1970s, or the Internet in the mid-1990s. Like these two, the Cloud is upon us: right now, today, in real time.

As consumers, our Cloud utilization is occurring seamlessly, with almost unwitting acceptance. Many of us today access the Cloud for movies, entertainment and applications, all on demand and all through a host of devices from our desktop PCs, to tablets and eBooks, to our phones. Our stores of photos, documents, music, movies – our personal data warehouses – all of these increasingly are "out there" as well.

For businesses, traditional notions of in-house data centers and centralized, internally-controlled IT infrastructure are falling precipitously to the performance and cost advantages of the Cloud.

The Cloud represents a brave new world for government IT management as well. For jurisdictions at all levels, the very recent and accepted trend to government-owned and/or controlled data center environments – thousands of them – is being eroded if not stopped in its tracks forthwith. Longstanding cultural biases to possess in order to best protect valuable and sensitive data treasuries now are being questioned. And for many a good reason. The simple truth is that the era of the government data center is surrendering first to consolidation, then reduction, perhaps even demise.

Again, all of this right now, today, in real time.

But what do we really know? How comfortable are we with putting data essential to everything from routine government operations to the most sensitive of government missions and challenges outside our control? *What is the Cloud?* Most in government, and almost anyone outside professional IT, correctly recognize the Cloud as a massive series of connections: hundreds of millions of devices connected to hundreds of thousands of servers, all of these connected to thousands of networks around the globe. It is amorphous. It is global. It facilitates billions of transactions 24x7x365. But whether one is an IT professional in or out of government, a technology policy wonk, or a manager at any level, few of us understand how the Cloud works, how data moves, is managed, or how it is secured.

On this important issue of security, we as government executives and practitioners often are assured of the Cloud's ability to protect important data, Big Data and small alike. But is it secure? It is out of our control so how can we be sure, 100 percent? Further, how do laws like the Federal Information Security Management Act (FISMA) apply to an amorphous IT infrastructure neither owned nor operated by government professionals?

Cloud reliability and performance metrics seem impressive, but how reliable are these for the public sector? Our government data requirements are unique both in their scale and in the often legislatively-driven processes by which they are governed. As Cloud applications explode across the public sector landscape,

CIOs and policy makers alike carry with them some uncertainty as to the long-term implications of this unstoppable technology transformation.

How do we in government buy Cloud services? And what happens to government IT budgets when usual capital requests move with limited review to the Operations and Maintenance (O&M) side of the ledger as they do with so many Cloud acquisitions? Acquisition and budget issues are complex enough; Cloud computing is out-side traditional boundaries of many existing acquisition processes and practices. These need to change, evolve and responsibly so.

Concerns and questions cited above, and others, are many and legitimate. The longstanding legal, regulatory and experience matrix governing public sector IT today needs to be reexamined, adjusted and changed where necessary. Reliable information is needed to ensure that changes in this matrix are made with haste and discipline certainly, but with wisdom as well.

In his book, Jim Sweeney makes a valuable, important and needed contribution to the Cloud discussion and debate swirling within the government IT sector. For practitioners and policy makers alike, Jim guides us first through a disciplined review of Cloud computing capabilities today, and what these are evolving toward in the very near, almost immediate future.

He addresses specific areas of greatest concern to government tech execs, security at the top of the list.

Most importantly, Jim invested time in meeting with government Cloud pioneers, early converts, practitioners, and advocates. Through very readable composition, Jim illustrates with each best-practice example an important aspect of Cloud computing. In doing so, he sets guide posts for us to consider, whether we are in IT acquisition, project design and management, enterprise IT management or even policy, regulatory or guidance development.

We are left with a clearer picture of the complex Cloud landscape, of strategy paths to move us from the legacy and the traditional to this new and promising technology phenomenon.

The road ahead for government and the Cloud is an exciting and important one, both for IT management and for the enhanced capabilities the Cloud promises us for new and improved government operations and services. Jim Sweeney shows us that blue skies for government Cloud are in the immediate forecast.

Right now, today, in real time.

Tom Davis
United States House of Representatives,
January 3, 1995 – November 24, 2008

Table Of Contents

Dedication   V
Acknowledgements   VI
Foreward   VII
Table of Figures Used in this Book   XIII
Chapter 1. Introduction   1
    A Book Was Born!   2
    The Goal Of This Book   2
    Before We Move On...   14
Chapter 2. Infrastructure as a Service Clouds (IaaS)   16
    The 5,000 foot view   19
    A Look At The Vendors And Their Offerings   20
    The Terremark IaaS Offering   30
    Summary   37
Chapter 3. Getting Started with AWS   39
Chapter 4. Jet Propulsion Laboratory (JPL) Case Study   58
Chapter 5. USA.gov Case Study   66
Chapter 6. Software as a Service Clouds (SaaS) for Email
and Collaboration   73
    Google   76
    Sonian   78
    Microsoft   82
    HyperOffice   85
Chapter 7. State of Minnesota Case Study   90
Chapter 8. SaaS Clouds for Other Uses   99
    GCE   109
    Summary   111
Chapter 9. US Department of Labor Case Study   112
Chapter 10. Platform as a Service Clouds (PaaS)   122
    Oracle   124
    Google App Engine   126
    Microsoft   130
Chapter 11. Getting Started with Google App Engine   134

Chapter 12. schoolconferences.com Case Study   143
Chapter 13. mytowngovernment.org Case Study   149
Chapter 14. Getting Started with Microsoft Windows Azure   158
Chapter 15. The City of Miami Case Study   165
Chapter 16. Private IaaS Clouds, Hybrid Clouds and
Community Clouds   172
  Private Clouds   *173*
  VI3 and vSphere   *175*
  VMware and the Private Cloud   *178*
  The Architecture   *181*
  The CA Private IaaS Cloud Offering   *182*
  Hybrid Clouds   *188*
  The Community Cloud   *190*
Chapter 17. Getting Started with vCloud   191
Chapter 18. Getting Started with CA   196
  CA Automation Suite for Clouds – The User's screens   *196*
  CA AppLogic   *205*
Chapter 19. Los Alamos National Labs Case Study   208
Chapter 20. Other Uses for the Cloud - Mechanical Turk   219
Chapter 21. John Hopkins University Case Study   222
Chapter 22. Summary   233
  Examples of Cloud   *234*
  Getting Started With Cloud   *236*
  What if I don't consider Cloud?   *241*
  How do I procure Cloud?   *242*
  Remember, Cloud is just one more tool   *243*
Appendix A. TechAmerica Cloud2 Commission Report   244
  Introduction/Purpose of Report   *248*
Appendix B. TechAmerica Cloud2SLG Report   252
Appendix C. GTSI Cloud Maturity Model   256
Index   CCLVII

Table of Figures Used in this Book

Figure 1-1: The NIST Cloud Framework   1

Figure 1-2: The Cloud Pyramid   9

Figure 1-3: An Alternate Version of the Cloud Pyramid   10

Figure 2-1: The SPI Model. Relating Services to Infrastructure   17

Figure 2-2: The Rackspace.com Website   35

Figure 2-3: Rackspace Ordering Page   36

Figure 2-4: The Account Activity Screen   37

Figure 3-1 The Amazon Web Service Home Page   40

Figure 3-2: AWS Signup Confirmation   41

Figure 3-3: Ready to Launch an EC2 Instance   41

Figure 3-4: Requesting the EC2 Instance   42

Figure 3-5: Selecting the Instance Details   43

Figure 3-6: Instances and Tags   43

Figure 3-7: Key Pair Creation   44

Figure 3-8: Security Groups and Firewall Rules   45

Figure 3-9: The Instance Creation Summary Screen   46

Figure 3-10: Creating an EC2 Volume   48

Figure 3-11: Creating a Volume   49

Figure 3-12: Results of our Volume Creation   49

Figure 3-13: The EC2 Dashboard   50

Figure 3-14: Starting EC2 Instances with CloudWatch   51

Figure 3-15: Enabling Monitoring   51

Figure 3-16: Instances with CloudWatch   52

Figure 3-17: CloudWatch   52

Figure 3-18: CloudWatch Metrics   53

Figure 3-19: Elastic Load Balancers   54

Figure 3-20: Load Balancer Creation Wizard   54

Figure 3-21: Creating the Load Balancer   55

Figure 3-22: Selecting the EC2 instances   56

Figure 3-23: ELB Creation - Summary Screen   56

Figure 3-24: Load Balancer Status   57

Figure 6-1: The SaaS Model   74

Figure 6-2: The Sonian Dashboard   80

Figure 6-3: The Search Screen   81

Figure 6-4: The Sonian Search Results Screen   81

Figure 6-5: The My Archive Screen   82

Figure 6-6: The My Archive Search Screen   83

Figure 6-7: The HyperOffice Suite   86

Figure 6-8: The HyperOffice Project and Calendar Screens   87

Figure 6-9: The HyperOffice Contact Screen   88

Figure 6-10: Reviews of the HyperOffice Product   89

Figure 8-1: Salesforce Welcome Screen   103

Figure 8-2: Salesforce.com Lead Insert Screen   103

Figure 8-3: New Lead Created   104

Figure 8-4: The Salesforce Chatter Screen   105

Figure 8-5: The Salesforce Reports Screen   105

Figure 8-6: The Salesforce Forecasts Screen   106

Figure 8-7: GCE SaaS Financial Management System - Modules   110

Figure 10-1: The PaaS Cloud   123

Figure 11-1: The Google App Engine Login Screen   135

Figure 11-2: The Google App Engine Verification Screen   135

Figure 11-3: Authentication Code Screen   135

Figure 11-4: Creating an Application   136

Figure 11-5: Application Registered   136

Figure 11-6: The Eclipse IDE for Java Developers   137

Figure 11-7: Creating a Web Application Project   137

Figure 11-8: My Eclipse Project   138

Figure 11-9: Java IDE with Sample Code Loaded   139

Figure 11-10: Running with the Emulator 139

Figure 11-11: Starting the Upload Process 140

Figure 11-12: Selecting the Project 141

Figure 11-13: The Log Screen of Eclipse After Deployment 141

Figure 11-14: It Works! 142

Figure 12-1: Schoolconferences.com 146

Figure 12-2: The Booking Page 146

Figure 12-3: School Sign up Page 147

Figure 13-1: The Town Calendar 154

Figure 13-2: Meeting History 154

Figure 13-3: Kiosk Mode 155

Figure 13-4: The Tutorial 155

Figure 13-5: Sign In Screen 156

Figure 14-1: Windows Azure Welcome Screen 159

Figure 14-2: Starting a New Project 159

Figure 14-3: The Modified Sample Code 160

Figure 14-4: Sample Application Test Result 160

Figure 14-5: Starting the Deployment Process 160

Figure 14-6: Log Screen Showing a Successful Deployment 161

Figure 14-7: Our Application Works! 161

Figure 14-8: Back to the Management Portal for Cleanup 161

Figure 14-9: Deleting the Application 162

Figure 14-10: A Review of the Cloud Service Models 163

Figure 15-1: The Miami 311 Application 169

Figure 16-1: The IaaS Cloud Model 173

Figure 16-2: GTSI IaaS Private Cloud 181

Figure 16-3: AppLogic in a Multiple Data Center Environment 186

Figure 17-1: The vCloud Login Screen 192

Figure 17-2: The GTSI Cloud 192

Figure 17-3: Administration Tab 193

Figure 17-4: The Manage and Monitor Tab 193

Figure 17-5: The GTSI vCenters 194

Figure 17-6: GTSI Hosts 194

Figure 17-7: GTSI Datastores 195

Figure 18-1: The User Login Screen 197

Figure 18-2: Starting the Reservation System 197

Figure 18-3: Virtual Machine Template 198

Figure 18-4: Selecting Additional Software Packages 198

Figure 18-5: Specifying the Virtual Machine Requirements 199

Figure 18-6: Specifying Dates 199

Figure 18-7: Almost Finished with the Request 200

Figure 18-8: The Confirmation Screen 200

Figure 18-9: The Status Screen 201

Figure 18-10: The Administrator's Screen 202

Figure 18-11: Resources Pools 202

Figure 18-12: Creating a New Resource Pool 203

Figure 18-13: System Images 201

Figure 18-14: The iPad Interface 204

Figure 18-15: Requesting Additional Time 204

Figure 18-16: A New Reservation 205

Figure 18-17: The CA AppLogic Application Editor 206

Figure 18-18: The Shell Console 207

Figure 18-19: The AppLogic Dashboard 207

Figure 19-1: Virtualization Challenges at LANL 210

Figure 19-2: Electrical Savings at LANL from Virtualization 211

Figure 19-3: The Los Alamos National Labs Self Service Portal 213

Figure 19-4: The "Create Server" Button on the LANL portal 214

Figure 19-5: Selecting and Sizing a Windows VM 215

Figure 19-6: The Real Savings on the LANL Portal 215

Figure 19-7: Selecting "Yellow" for on Premise 216

Figure 19-8: Going "Green" 216

Figure 19-9 Multiple Service Levels   216
Figure 19-10: Infrastructure on Demand Management Console   215
Figure 21-1: Map of Various Arabic Dialects   228
Figure 21-2: Mechanical Turk Home Screen   230
Figure 21-3: Mechanical Turk User Registration   230
Figure 21-4: The Requester Page   231
Figure 21-5: Naming Your Project   231
Figure 21-6: Project Category   232
Appendix B: Global IT Mega Trends for Mega Business Benefits 253

CHAPTER
1

Introduction

My true introduction to Cloud came while serving on the TechAmerica Cloud2 commission. This commission, formed at the request of then–CIO Vivek Kundra, attempted to speed the adoption of Cloud in federal government. Sterling Phillips, the CEO of GTSI, was one of the commissioners along with 70 other industry representatives. Once I accepted Sterling Phillips' offer to become his deputy on the commission, I was immediately propelled into a series of meetings with industry heavyweights surrounding the issues of Cloud, the slow adoption of Cloud within federal, state and local governments, and the creation of a whole new set of recommendations that Vivek Kundra brought to government. I also participated as a co-chair of the Budget, Acquisition and Execution sub-committee. There were many committee members who had horror stories of government attempts to acquire Cloud services, some of which made their way into the recommendations for the final report. The final report is fascinating reading for anyone in the public sector who is interested in Cloud Computing; you'll find the Foreward and the Introduction of the report in Appendix A. The full report can be downloaded from the TechAmerica web site at www.techamerica.org. I was subsequently asked to serve as a commissioner on the state and local-focused Cloud2 commission in the fall and winter of 2011. Again, the findings are quite revealing. Because this book is aimed at public sector of all types, I have included the Executive Summary Appendix B.

Needless to say, by this point, I had become totally immersed in Cloud. I began to identify the issues that had become recurring themes: confusion over the many different types of Cloud, how they operate, and the benefits of each.

A Book Was Born!

It occurred to me that what was really missing was a book that addressed the various types of Clouds, the benefits, the architectures and a set of examples that potential Cloud customers could use as a resource for developing ideas for using Cloud offerings within their own agency.

The Goal Of This Book

The goal of this book is to clear up the most common misconceptions about Cloud and provide answers to some of the most commonly-asked questions about this technology.

But Why A Book On Cloud Specifically?

The answer is simple: because there is so much misunderstanding about Cloud. Almost everyone has an idea of what Cloud is, yet very few people see the whole picture. Misinformation on the internet only exacerbates the problem. That misunderstanding leads to a multitude of excuses for not thinking "Cloud first." And to complicate matters even further, the misinformation coming from non-Cloud vendors who think they just have to re-label every product they have as "Cloud" muddies the waters even more!

Why A Case Study Book On Cloud?

When I was a child, I learned best by example. Actually, I still do. I think most people learn best that way, especially when they are trying to learn something that is somewhat complicated. To illustrate my point, have you ever tried to learn the game of chess? Better yet, have you ever tried to teach someone the game? It is no doubt a great game – the so-called "Game of Kings." Even though I have never taken the time to become very good at playing chess, the various moves, openings, and strategy all fascinate me. But learning even basic chess for the first time is time consuming and frustrating. Learning the pieces and their different moves is enough to drive anyone crazy! Without real world examples, you are lucky if someone sticks around long enough to hear you explain all the pieces and their move combinations before they throw in the towel. But get them through that, and challenge them to play a few games...and, before you know it, your chess student begins to see the strategy of the game and how they might be able to use it to formulate their own winning moves. That is why many chess books have examples of games played by the greatest masters of all time.

The same is true with this book. We are going to take a look at what Cloud computing is (*and what it isn't*), and then look at several case studies at all levels of the public sector and examine their use of Cloud. We will examine the problem that inspired them to consider a Cloud solution. We will also look at why that decision was made, i.e., what were the business, technical – and yes, even political – drivers that led to that decision. We'll examine the architecture they selected and why. We'll look at the challenges they faced in moving to the Cloud, both technical and non-technical. And finally, we'll look at their results. Do they consider their use of Cloud to be successful? Are they contemplating any other uses for Cloud? We are going to look at every phase of the problem, the decision-making process, their challenges and their plans for expansion.

Aren't There Enough Books On Cloud Already?

Actually, there are hundreds of books in print about Cloud technology. Several are from vendors of Cloud solutions trying to convince you that their particular brand of Cloud is the absolute best for everyone. And there are those from industry pundits espousing Cloud for everyone.

But we are not "everyone." This book is aimed squarely at IT professionals employed by federal, state and local governments. Several of you are already looking at Cloud. Some of you have looked at it and dismissed it. And some of you have wholeheartedly embraced it at one level or another.

Many federal, state and local agencies are using Cloud in various forms today. Many of you wonder if Cloud is right for you. And many who harbor a number of misconceptions about Cloud are quite frankly nervous about, or unwilling to move, to a technology so new and different.

Not every organization will find an immediate need for Cloud. Certainly no agency would move their entire infrastructure to the Cloud immediately. But, I think everyone can find something in their organization that would benefit from moving to the Cloud. Maybe it's a highly scalable environment. Maybe it's a resource constraint issue. Or maybe it's just a budgeting (CapEx vs OpEx) problem that can be solved with the Cloud.

Which brings me back to the reason why I was compelled to write a book on Cloud: to keep federal state and local IT departments

from taking 3-5 years to adopt something that could make a posi-
tive impact to their organization now!

So that you don't misconstrue this book as a cleverly-disguised
sales pitch, I don't currently work for one of the Cloud providers.
I work for a reseller/integrator (GTSI Corp.) that resells and offers
services on many different Cloud providers. My company specifically develops service offerings that can assist federal, state and
local government customers in assessing if Cloud is right for all
or part of their infrastructure. We help these agencies develop
plans to move to the Cloud (either by using a public provider or
by developing their own agency-wide Cloud architecture).

This may seem like a lot of gobbledy-gook now – but I hope to
fix that as you move through the book! My aim is to show you
how others have made the decision to use Cloud in one way
or another for all or part of their IT infrastructure. I want you to
understand your options and choose the best Cloud solution (or
make an informed choice not to use Cloud) for your particular
organization and application with your particular needs. Maybe,
like playing chess for the very first time, this book will give you
some strategies for your own organization.

Hasn't There Been Enough Hype About Cloud Already?

It seems as though you can't turn a page in a magazine, search
for anything relating to IT, or even open your email without reading, hearing, or seeing something about Cloud. Everyone in the
federal, state and local marketplace seems to have a different
idea of what Cloud really is. Is it Salesforce.com? Or VMware? Or
Amazon? Google? Or how 'bout Microsoft and their email-and-
collaboration-in-the-Cloud service? Or insert-your-latest-vendor-
presentation here. Suffice it to say that there are a lot of offerings
out there. And there are many, many vendors who are calling
what they do "Cloud" just because *it is* the latest buzzword. In
many cases, their offering is either a very small piece of the
Cloud puzzle or not Cloud at all.

We are not only going to explore the various types of Clouds and relate them to vendor offerings, but show real examples from real government customers. We are also going to use these examples to demonstrate the various types of Cloud offerings that are available at the moment.

Types Of Clouds Available Today:
So let's get started. There are three established service models for Cloud:[1]

Infrastructure as a Service Cloud (IaaS). The capability provided to the consumer is to provision processing, storage, networks, and other fundamental computing resources where the consumer is able to deploy and run arbitrary software, which can include operating systems and applications. The consumer does not manage or control the underlying Cloud infrastructure but has control over operating systems, storage, and deployed applications; and possibly limited control of select networking components (e.g., host firewalls). Terremark, (now owned by Verizon) is a great example of an IaaS Cloud. Amazon Web Services (commonly referred to as AWS) is also a great example of an IaaS Cloud. We'll cover a lot more of IaaS Cloud architectures, features, advantages and benefits in Chapter 2.

Software as a Service Cloud (SaaS). The capability provided to the consumer is to use the provider's applications running on a Cloud infrastructure. The applications are accessible from various client devices through either a thin client interface, such as a web browser (e.g., web-based email), or a program interface. The consumer does not manage or control the underlying Cloud infrastructure including network, servers, operating systems, storage, or even individual application capabilities, with the possible exception of limited user-specific application configuration settings. We'll discuss this and many other scenarios as well as the architectures, features, advantages and benefits in Chapters 6 and 8.

1 NIST Special Publication 800-145, "The NIST Definition of Cloud Computing", Peter Mell & Timothy Grance.

Platform as a Service Cloud (PaaS). The capability provided to the consumer is to deploy onto the Cloud infrastructure consumer-created or acquired applications created using pro- gramming languages, libraries, services, and tools supported by the provider. The consumer does not manage or control the underlying Cloud infrastructure including network, servers, operating systems, or storage, but has control over the de- ployed applications and possibly configuration settings for the application-hosting environment. You might think of the Google App Engine environment or the Microsoft Windows Azure plat- form. We will look at these in detail starting in Chapter 10.

In addition, NIST has delineated four accepted deployment models for Cloud:[2]

Private Cloud. The Cloud infrastructure is provisioned for exclusive use by a single organization comprising multiple consumers (e.g., business units). It may be owned, managed, and operated by the organization, a third party, or some com- bination of them, and it may exist on or off premises. While this has traditionally been an accepted form of Cloud deployment, this model is currently not in favor with most experts today. It is unfortunate that this model has somehow become the default way of thinking for many federal government agencies, as well as for some state and local governments. I'll discuss this trend in chapter 16 and why I think private Clouds are not the types of Clouds that government could and should be using.

Community Cloud. The Cloud infrastructure is provisioned for exclusive use by a specific community of consumers from organizations that have shared concerns (e.g., mission, security requirements, policy, and compliance considerations). It may be owned, managed, and operated by one or more of the organiza- tions in the community, a third party, or some combination of them, and it may exist on or off premises. I really have not seen a good example of this in use in the public sector.

2 Ibid

In doing research for this book, I saw a reference to GovCloud. com[3] as a community Cloud offering exclusively for federal, state and local governments. In reality, however, GovCloud.com is a company owned by Rackspace. It is simply a vendor selling Cloud enablement services.

Public Cloud. The Cloud infrastructure is provisioned for open use by the general public. It may be owned, managed, and operated by a business, academic, or government organization, or some combination of them. It exists on the premises of the Cloud provider. Google®, Amazon Web Services®, Salesforce. com®, and Terremark™ are all public Clouds. Anyone can sign up for their services and begin using and paying for these services immediately.

Hybrid Cloud. The Cloud infrastructure is a composition of two or more distinct Cloud infrastructures (private, community, or

NIST CLOUD DEFINITION FRAMEWORK

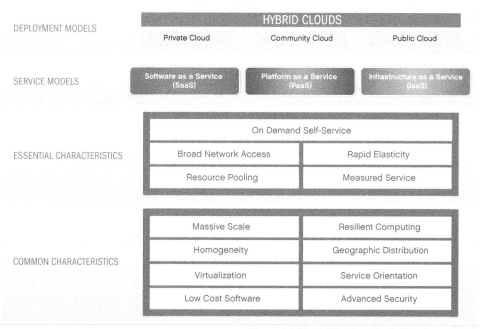

Figure 1-1: The NIST Cloud Definition Framework

3 Not to be confused with GovCloud (US) an offering from Amazon Web Services.

public) that remain unique entities, but are bound together by standardized or proprietary technology that enables data and application portability (e.g., Cloud bursting or load balancing between Clouds). Earlier I mentioned that private Clouds are being hotly debated as a good example of Cloud computing. That is because many IT professionals in the public sector are looking at them solely as a way to "check the box" and not evaluate a real public Cloud offering. Hybrid Clouds are an excellent way for the government to have a private Cloud which interfaces to a public Cloud and allows the IT professional to move applications and data between the two.

The NIST (National Institute of Standards and Technology) Cloud Definition Framework, in figure 1-1 explains the various service models, and deployment models as well as the characteristics, (essential and common) that are integral parts of each Cloud.

This puts Cloud into a nice package. Unfortunately, at least from a conceptual standpoint, not all of the Cloud fits into these nice easy graphics. For example, you can have a SaaS model whereby the software vendor runs his software (and any accompanying services necessary to deliver the software to the user) on top of an IaaS Cloud vendor! So you can easily have Cloud Service Models stacked on top of one another as in figure 1-2:

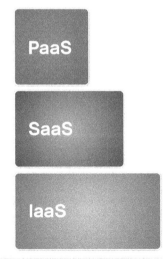

As you can see from figure 1-2, this complicates things when trying to explain Cloud for the first time. You can even go crazy and turn the top of the pyramid upside down as in figure 1-3, though the infrastructure is always underlying everything. As we look at each of the various Cloud models, you will see why figure 1-2 and figure 1-3 make perfect sense from both the vendor's and the customer's perspective.

Figure 1-2: The Cloud Pyramid

"Can't We Do Things The Old Way?"

I love this question. Or rather, the corollary of it. "Cloud computing is just a phase that will pass. I'm sure we can wait this out like we waited out so many other new trends that have come and gone."

It reminds me of the scene from the movie "Other People's Money." In the movie Lawrence Garfield, played by Danny DeVito, is targeting the takeover of the New England Cable and Wire Company. Standing there in front of all of the stockholders and the President of New England Wire and Cable, including James Stewart as company president Andrew Jorgenson, Garfield said:

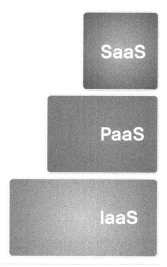

Figure 1-3: An Alternate version of the Cloud Pyramid

"...We're dead alright. We're just not broke. And you know the surest way to go broke? Keep getting an increasing share of a shrinking market. Down the tubes. Slow but sure. You know, at one time there must've been dozens of companies making buggy whips. And I'll bet the last company around was the one that made the best goddamn buggy whip you ever saw. Now how would you have liked to have been a stockholder in that company? You invested in a business and this business is dead. Let's have the intelligence, let's have the decency to sign the death certificate, collect the insurance, and invest in something with a future."

Garfield was trying to tell the owners of New England Wire and Cable that the days of manufacturing copper cable were over and, while you might be the best manufacturer left of all the others that had changed, grown or gone out of business, you weren't going to be in business long if you didn't progress. At the end, opposing lawyer Kate Sullivan charges in on a virtual white horse and transforms the company into one that makes air bags, the major component of which is copper wire. We are led to believe that the "new" New England Cable and Wire – errr...Airbag Company – went on to make record profits for themselves and the shareholders, and that the two co-stars went on to a life of eternal bliss.

But enough about bliss...The company took an old technology, re-tooled it, and with additional training for their employees, became a new, profitable, agile company with a product that is needed now more than ever. "But we are not companies," I can hear you saying. "We're government." True, but the lesson is still the same. Staying the same for the sake of staying the same – especially in an era of shrinking budgets - doesn't improve IT services to the organization, it doesn't help the taxpayer and it sure doesn't do anything for your career in IT!

My goal is to show you, through the use of case studies, the benefits of Cloud, the various ways in which others are implementing Cloud to solve their public sector problems, and how those IT departments are now more agile and can offer better services for their customers.

And they are doing it against all of the current objections that are out there!

The most prevalent objection to migrating to Cloud technology is "we're different."

I have heard that statement at every federal government customer meeting I have attended for the past 15 years. You are **not** different. Seriously; you are not different. Your problems are very much the same as your brethren in other agencies. You have the same concerns about security, the same "special" circumstances, the same fears, and the same trepidations about new technology that makes your problem...well, the same.

Or how about this objection: "We have sensitive data." Is there any piece of data today that is not considered sensitive? Yet we have data lying around on laptops or accessed via non-secure internet connections, or worse, residing on tablets, PDAs or other mobile devices that aren't secure, aren't backed up, or even patched to the highest security level. When you access your IRA account or your bank account – is this not sensitive data? Of course it is. What about the national database that is accessed by state and local police when you are stopped for just about any moving violation? It's the same database that is accessed from all sorts of different devices over many different types of unsecure connections (including unsecured radios which anyone can receive with $10.00 worth of parts).

Others have conquered their issues around security and you can too. Some people now consider the Cloud more secure than their environment. Here's a great example. I recently participated in a demonstration of an online charity that is hosted in the Cloud. The first question was asked by a government IT worker about security. I loved the presenter's answer: "It is part of the Cloud offering and we let them handle that. They are the professionals and they provide this service for many, many of their customers. It's much more secure than if we implemented it ourselves!"

Cloud is not for everything or everyone. It's not right for every scenario and every type of data. At this time, I do not believe that there are secure solutions for putting classified data in a public Cloud. We may get there very soon, especially considering the pace of technology development these days. Beyond that, I truly believe that there are great applications in each agency that could take advantage of some kind of Cloud offering.

As you will see, your fellow IT professionals in federal as well as state and local governments are successfully using various Cloud offerings available today.

Can't We Build Our Own Internal Cloud And Be Done With It?

Then you'll be able to "check the box" that you have implemented Cloud and everyone will get off your backs, right? Well, not exactly. But it's the kind of faulty logic that's prevalent today. While internal Clouds may very well be appropriate for some applications or may be part of a good architecture, they are not the end-all and be-all of Cloud. They may even make a great piece of the puzzle in a Hybrid Cloud scenario (see Chapter 16).

Even if you already have a well-architected, virtualized infrastructure and you overlay some Cloud software that allows your users to perform self-provisioning and chargeback to create a very simple IaaS Cloud (Infrastructure as a Service), you are still missing many of the attributes of a well-architected IaaS Cloud. There are several reasons why this is not Cloud:

- For one, you cannot take advantage of the elasticity of Cloud; i.e. the ability to rapidly provision and de-provision (and correspondingly, pay for and stop paying for) an asset. In a private Cloud, you don't have the elasticity which is essential to Cloud, so therefore (with certain exceptions) it's a pretty poor excuse for "getting around the checkbox" and not looking at a potentially better way of doing business today.

- You are also not taking advantage of another great advantage of Cloud computing: no upfront costs. When you move to a true Cloud environment there are no upfront costs. Period. You pay for only what you use at that time. If you are building your own private Cloud from scratch, you don't have this luxury. You have huge upfront costs with which you need to be concerned. If you are overlaying Cloud management software on top of your already-virtualized infrastructure, that might be one thing, but huge upfront investments are not part of the Cloud.

- Cloud providers today have already built their Clouds with all of the interfaces into the existing systems management tools that you already own and use. This means that you can switch management tools on a whim, and the Cloud will still work with them! Will you have that in your environment by overlaying

Cloud provisioning and chargeback on top of your virtualized infrastructure?

- And finally, the Cloud vendors have built-in, preprogrammed API (Application Programming Interfaces), languages, operating systems and databases to offer you ultimate flexibility in your environment. Can you truly make the same point about a virtualized infrastructure on which you added some Cloud software?

I am not saying that all private Clouds are bad. In fact, they are often the place where people start with a vision towards moving into a hybrid environment in the future. That's a good thing. But in and of itself, with very few exceptions, a private Cloud is not really the answer. We really need to stop using "We are building our own internal, private Cloud" as the excuse to keep us from evaluating real Cloud solutions – and the benefits that they offer – for some or all of the environment!

Cloud really needs to be evaluated by the service that you are offering to your customers and not at the agency-wide level. For example, a private Cloud which will morph into a hybrid Cloud for test and development might be a good thing, but there are great SaaS solutions for email, collaboration, CRM and ERP services which should be evaluated for those services. By the time you are finished with this book, I hope you will realize that there are a variety of options out there for you, that each should be evaluated according to the service you want to offer, and through the case studies, that others have gone before you and have already paved the way!

Before We Move On...

I'd like a word with all of the vendors out there. You cannot just add the words "as a service" to your product and have it become a Cloud product. Pizza-as-a-Service is not a Cloud, it's your local pizza shop. Automobile-as-a-service is not a Cloud, it's a taxi. Since marketing companies are constantly, and irritatingly,

adding those three words to their tag lines in the hope of cash-
ing in on the Cloud hype, I hope by the time you finish this book,
you will be better prepared to tell those vendors "thanks, but no
thanks" when you find that what they are selling is really pizza
delivery or taxis – and not truly Cloud.

So there you have it. Another book on Cloud. This one hopefully,
a little different – a little more relevant – than the others because
it is focused strictly on federal, state and local government IT
personnel, their users, and their particular needs. A book that will
show you examples of how your peers in federal, state and local
IT are already successfully using some form of Cloud and plan to
expand their usage.

Infrastructure as a Service Clouds (IaaS)

Perhaps the easiest of the Cloud offerings to understand is the Infrastructure as a Service (Iaas) Cloud. IaaS Cloud is pronounced I-a-a-S. There appears to be no acronym pronunciation as with Saas, which is pronounced "sass," and PaaS which is pronounced "pass."

An IaaS Cloud offering is simple to understand because it is infrastructure, like the servers, switches and storage that you already own and use today. Infrastructure that you can use just like it was yours. And of course, pay for it when you are using it – and stop paying for it when you no longer need it.

This is somewhat akin to buying a server, using it for 3 minutes, or 6 days or 9 weeks or even 18 months until after your development effort is complete, and then returning it to the manufacturer for the value of the server at that time. Or using 60TB of NAS storage as backup for your environment when your disaster recovery data center is hit by a natural disaster and you no longer have the use of that datacenter for the next 24 months while it is being repaired.

There are many versions of the chart below, but I think this one best explains the differences between the three main types of Clouds that are available today.

As you can see from figure 2-1 below, the IaaS Cloud provides the most components for the user to manage. Infrastructure-as-

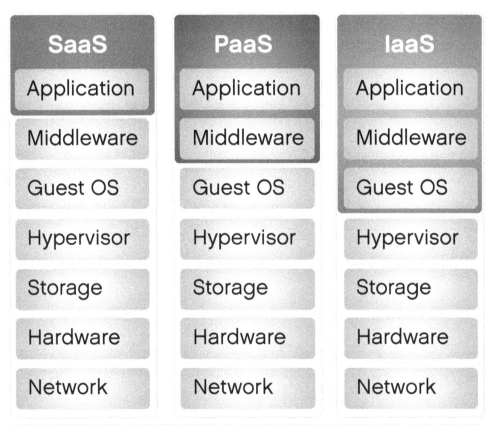

Figure 2-1: The SPI Model. Relating Services to infrastructure
Securing the Cloud, Vic (J.K.) Winkler. Syngress Press ©2011

a-Service Cloud not only presents the servers and storage, but also the corresponding network settings for the user (or administrator) to control. In contrast, the SaaS Cloud presents only the software to the user while hiding everything below it. The PaaS Cloud presents only those layers necessary for software development.

Here are a couple of great use cases for IaaS Clouds:

1. Let's assume you have researched which servers you want. You have spec'd the architecture out and believe you need 5 web servers, 3 application servers and 2 redundant DB servers. You have budgeted for all of these systems and the budget has been approved. However, before you can make the purchase, something with a higher priority comes up and you no longer have the budget to purchase these servers. You now have nothing on which to develop your application or perform the testing of that application, let alone the resources to move it into production. Perhaps taking advantage of an IaaS Cloud to "rent" the servers and storage that you need for the time that you need it, and no more, is a good option for you.

2. Suppose you are developing a new application and have no idea how popular this application will be. For example, you are developing a new web-based application that many users could potentially use, but how many really will? And will they all use it at the same time? This problem presents an interesting conundrum for the developer. How many servers do you need? Do you need the same number at all times? Do you design the hardware architecture for worst case scenario, purchasing 20 servers, when in reality you might only need 10 servers on average, with 2 servers hosting your application in the middle of the night and maybe 15 servers for peak usage, say between 5 and 7 pm EST? Or maybe you put this application in an IaaS Cloud and let the auto-scaling feature automatically (within your bounds, of course) add and delete additional resources as user demand ebbs and flows.

3. Or, let's say you are a data analyst. You have a very large dataset. You need to perform some kind of analysis on that data. You are currently running the algorithm against this dataset and it takes you 4 days to complete each run. Why not tweak the application a little to run in a distributed environment? Then you could load your data into the IaaS Cloud, spin up 50 servers at once and have the job completed in under an hour. Then of course, release those servers back to the Cloud having only paid for them for the time that you used them.

In all of these examples, an IaaS Cloud architecture could provide a cost-effective and viable solution. While every vendor architects their IaaS Cloud offering differently, they all have a few things in common:

1. **Servers** that you can treat as your own for as long as you need them. Note that I did not say "virtual" servers. Some IaaS Cloud providers actually offer physical servers and you load as many virtual machines on top of them as you can fit onto that particular server. On the other hand, some only provide virtual machines.

2. **Storage Capacity** that you can use. You are charged for the amount of storage you use for the time that you use it. It is important to note that the type of storage you are provided may not be the exact type you are using, so you need to determine if the storage architecture you are offered will work for your application.

3. **Supporting Network Infrastructure** over which you have at least some control. While you may not be able to edit every single setting of the switch, you do have a moderate amount of control over the network support infrastructure as it relates to your specific Cloud servers and storage.

The 5,000 foot view

An easy way to think about Infrastructure as a Service Cloud is to think of it as a logical extension of your data centers. Perhaps a budget shortfall has prevented you from purchasing additional servers. Or maybe a tech refresh didn't come through as anticipated. While moving applications to the Cloud may have its pitfalls, you decide to use servers and storage from the Cloud for a short period of time. In this particular case, it is necessary that you manage the servers and have access to the servers as though they were part of your logical infrastructure even though they are not part of your physical infrastructure in your data center. This is a Virtual Private Cloud.

In other cases you may want to physically separate the hardware at the Cloud provider from your current infrastructure. For example, you have a short-term situation where you need servers for three months to crunch all of the data that's been in a database for the past 10 years. Depending on the level of data sensitivity or classification of the data they are processing, these servers may not need to be physically located inside your data center. In fact, for your purposes, they really do not need to be part of your physical infrastructure or managed as part of your local infrastructure. These servers exist only for the time frame it takes to complete the task and then returned to the Cloud pool.

A Look At The Vendors And Their Offerings

One of the confusing things about Cloud, even something as simple as an IaaS Cloud, is that everyone seems to implement it just a little differently. This makes comparing Cloud offerings from multiple vendors a somewhat difficult and arduous task. In many cases, it's helpful to understand their history in order to understand where they are today. We are going to look at three IaaS vendors, considering their architectures, basic constructs, and the features that really make them stand out from their competitors.

Amazon Web Services (AWS) grew out of the SOA infrastructure that Amazon needed to support its book reseller business. Terremark and Rackspace both started out as co-location facilities. In fact, both of them still have these offerings in addition to standard IaaS Cloud services. Not that this is necessarily a bad thing, but it means that their models differ from Amazon Cloud Services.

What about Cloud providers in Europe and Asia? Many of the US vendors mentioned above also have facilities in Europe or Asia, but there are also many other good companies with strong IaaS offerings serving these markets. An exhaustive comparison of all of these vendors would take the entire book, so I have selected a representative three from the United States. And let's not forget South America. In December 2011, Amazon announced a new region located in Sao Paulo, Brazil!

Amazon Web Services

AWS is a lot of things to a lot of people. In this case, when examining a simple IaaS Cloud, we are only dealing with a very small portion of the Amazon Web Services Cloud, specifically, Compute, Storage, Network, and Database. We'll also consider some of the complementary features that can be used within their IaaS Cloud offering: load balancing, Amazon's Virtual Private Cloud, Cloud Watch, and even something called "spot instances." But as your requirements become more complicated, there are many other features, all loosely coupled, that you may want to consider. The Amazon services together comprise an IaaS Cloud. Elastic Cloud 2.0 (EC2) and its ancillary products are the only portions that some IaaS vendors provide. The additional features not often found in other IaaS Cloud providers' offerings are really what distinguish the Amazon IaaS Cloud from others in the pack. Some people mistake this for Platform-as-a-Service (PaaS) Cloud but that is not the case. When we discuss all of the development tools that are available in the PaaS Cloud (chapter 10), I think you'll see and understand the difference.

Although we cannot look at every aspect of the AWS Cloud, in Chapter 3 we'll show you how to get started step by step with AWS. Let's examine the compute functionality first.

The Amazon EC2 Cloud is divided into regions. In United States, there are two regions called US East and US West. Around the world there are four other regions: the EU region located in Ireland, the Asia-Pacific region located in Singapore, the Asia-Pacific region located in Tokyo, Japan, and the recently-launched Sao Paulo region in Brazil. Since we are focused on the public sector, it is especially important to note here that **you can specify** where your virtual machines and the associated data are stored. In other words, if you don't want your data stored outside of United States borders, you can specify either the US West or the US East regions. Within each region, there are one or more availability zones. For those of you located in and around the Washington, D.C. area, there are at least three availability zones in the US East region. So with Amazon, you have complete control of the zone/region in which your data will reside, a very important feature if you are dealing with data that is a little more sensitive than normal.

There are several concepts that I want to touch on briefly before we discuss how to use the AWS Cloud. The first (and this will help you as you architect and troubleshoot applications), is that Amazon makes a distinction between the layers they control, and the layers that you control, as in the table below:

Things that Amazon Controls	Things that Users Control
The Facilities	Operating System
The Physical Security	The Application
The Physical Infrastructure	The Security Groups
The Network Infrastructure	The OS Firewalls
The Virtualization Infrastructure	Network Configuration
	Account Management

Secondly, in an effort to attract new customers, AWS has received a number of certifications, among them:
• SAS70 Type II Audit
• ISO 27001 Certification

- Payment Card Industry Data Security Standard (PCI DSS) Level 1 Service Provider

In addition, customers have already deployed various compliant applications, including those that meet:
- Sarbanes-Oxley (SOX)
- HIPAA (healthcare)
- FISMA moderate
- DIACAP MAC III Sensitive IATO

For additional security, AWS recommends that all customers use SSL/TLS for data in transit and that customers encrypt all data at rest using something like BitLocker™ or TrueCrypt.™

An important distinction that Amazon makes when talking about the Cloud is the difference between designing for an internal data center versus designing for the Cloud. When designing for your internal data center, you incorporate built-in redundancy within your entire architecture with no single points of failure. In the Amazon Cloud, however, you architect assuming that things *will* fail, but that you can recover quickly. That is not to say that there are no built-in failsafe features within the AWS system, but rather that there is a fundamental design difference when design-ing for cloud. This is the entire philosophy of the Amazon Web Services Cloud.

So let's talk about EC2. As we will show in the coming chapters, an EC2 instance is a virtual machine running within a specified region and zone. You launch instances with a variety of operating systems, load them with your custom application environment, manage your network's access permissions, and run your image using as many or few systems as you desire.

AWS has pre-configured, templated images from which you can select to get up and running immediately. These include Microsoft™ operating systems, various Linux operating systems and even some not-so-common operating systems. Or you can create an Amazon Machine Image (AMI) containing your applications, libraries, data, and associated configuration settings. Of course, you only pay for the resources that you actually consume, like instance-hours or data transferred.

There are several different types of instances in the AWS Cloud:

- On-Demand Instances – On-Demand Instances let you pay for compute capacity by the hour with no long-term commitments. You do not need to understand your applications utilization. You do not need to do any planning, purchasing, or maintaining hardware.

- Reserved Instances – Reserved Instances give you the option to make a low, one-time payment for each instance you want to reserve and in turn receive a significant discount on the hourly charge for that instance. There are three Reserved Instance types (Light, Medium, and Heavy Utilization) that enable you to balance the amount you pay upfront with your effective hourly price.

- Spot Instances – Spot Instances allow customers to bid on unused Amazon EC2 capacity and run those instances for as long as their bid exceeds the current Spot Price. The Spot Price changes periodically based on supply and demand, and customers whose bids meet or exceed it gain access to the available Spot Instances. If you have flexibility in when your applications can run, Spot Instances can significantly lower your Amazon EC2 costs. See the AWS web site for more details on Spot Instances.

We've examined servers, or instances, in the Amazon Cloud. Now let's talk briefly about storage. There are two kinds of storage available with Amazon: EBS, or Elastic Block Storage, and S3, or Simple Storage Service. EBS is block storage that you use as additional "drives" for your virtual machines or instances. We will see how to create these in the next chapter, Getting Started with AWS. S3 storage is storage for the Internet. What I really like about it, beside the fact that it is inexpensive, is that:

   a. Each object is stored in a bucket and retrieved via a unique, developer-assigned key.

   b. A bucket of storage can be created in any region you want and it never leaves that region unless you specify that it should.

   c. You can write, read, and delete objects containing from 1 byte to 5 terabytes of data each. The number of objects you can store is unlimited.

From a security perspective, AWS has you covered too. S3 is:

   a. Designed to provide 99.999999999% durability and 99.99% availability of objects over a given year.

   b. Designed to sustain the concurrent loss of data in two facilities.

But there is one additional feature that I really love about S3. Each bucket of data is addressable via a URL. Now I can store my personal web page, jimsweeney.info, in its own bucket. I simply use my domain name registrar to redirect requests from www.jim-sweeney.info to the URL where my S3 objects are stored. As long as I have an index.html file, everything will display normally. I can also turn on another feature called CloudFront which allows me to push my web content in my bucket to the AWS edge locations for faster delivery of content to you. Perhaps this is why Netflix uses the AWS S3 storage as their method for streaming movies to homes around the world!

There is one more feature that is essential to any three-tier application model: the database server. As you might expect, Amazon has a solution for that, too. It's the Amazon RDS or Relational Database Service, a web service that makes it easy to set up, operate, and scale a relational database in the Cloud. It provides cost-efficient and resizable capacity while managing time-consuming database administration tasks, freeing you up to focus on your applications and business.

Amazon RDS gives you access to the capabilities of a familiar Microsoft SQL Server® or Oracle® database. What this means for you is that the code, applications, and tools you already use in your existing architectures with your existing databases can be used with Amazon RDS. There's another advantage too. Amazon automatically patches the database software and backs up your database, storing the backups for as long as you need them, and enabling a very granular point-in-time recovery. You don't have to worry about any of that. You can even use replication for enhanced availability (just like in your infrastructure – no single point of failure). And again, there are no up-front investments required. You pay only for the resources you use.

Finally, there is a new database option with AWS. It's called DynamoDB. Amazon DynamoDB is a fully managed NoSQL data-base service that provides:

a. Fast and predictable performance
b. Seamless scalability

Using DynamoDB you can launch a new table, or scale up or down the requested capacity for that table without downtime or performance degradation. In addition, you gain visibility into resource utilization and performance metrics that are unavailable with other products.

Ancillary Features of AWS

Before we leave our discussion of AWS, there are a couple of additional features included with the AWS system that are not strictly part of an IaaS infrastructure, but are tightly coupled with the IaaS system.

Once you have created an EC2 environment, the ancillary features that simplify standing up, controlling, and monitor-ing an IT Infrastructure as a Service Cloud are the things that distinguish Amazon from its competitors. (And many strictly

IaaS Cloud providers do not have them). Let's take a look at a couple of them:

- **EC2 Elastic Load Balancer.** When you are contemplating a move to the Cloud, you first consider moving your Web servers because they are often the easiest workloads conceptually to move. But you probably don't just have one Web server. You probably have several Web servers with some method in place to load balance the traffic between these servers. AWS provides much the same kind of service, except there's no hardware for you to worry about. To Amazon, a load balancer is just another feature of the EC2 Cloud that you can choose to turn on among a discrete number of servers. This doesn't just apply to Web servers, although it is the most common use for the load balancing service. Any set of EC2 virtual machine instances can be load balanced using this feature. It is part of the EC2 system – you simply enable it and tell it to point to the server instances that you want it to balance. It's really that easy.

- **EC2 CloudWatch.** This feature collects information about the performance of each of your EC2 instances. Amazon CloudWatch monitors resources such as Amazon EC2, load balancers, Elastic Block Store volumes and Amazon RDS DB instances. It also monitors custom metrics generated by your applications with just a little setup on your part. With Amazon CloudWatch, you gain system-wide visibility into resource utilization, application performance, and operational health. It's a separate tab on the main screen but it's easy to find. Like everything they do, it's simple to turn on, configure and begin using. There are also numerous free metrics that you can turn on and monitor (these monitor every 5 minutes). There is an additional set that monitor every minute for a small fee. The EBS volumes have several metrics that monitor your storage at five minute intervals, the load balancers measure metrics at one minute intervals, and the RDS has over 11 metrics that look into your database and record usage-type statistics.

- **EC2 AutoScale.** The EC2 Cloudwatch feature is interesting enough in its own right, but it gets better. Based on the defined triggers that you set up, the EC2 Auto Scale feature uses the data collected by CloudWatch to automatically add additional EC2 instances when the load is heavy and scale them down when traffic is light. For example, when the US Census Bureau announces this year's version of the statistical book, an annual compilation of statistics on the social political and economic status of the United States and the world, traffic for that site may spike because of all the researchers who are anxiously awaiting that data for their economic research. Wouldn't it be great to have the AWS system automatically scale up additional web servers as needed during this critical time when new data is released and then scale them back down when the demand wanes?

Here's another example of the auto scale feature. Let's suppose you are an organization that has a standard three-tier application with a database server, a couple of application servers, and three Web servers, all being load balanced automatically using the AWS features. Everything is working great until you make the front page of your local newspaper or appear on the Oprah Winfrey show. While you are sitting at the dinner table watching Oprah to see how your company fares, demand from other viewers watching the program is causing your Web servers to be overloaded with traffic. Automatically, and without your knowledge or interaction, the AWS auto scale feature notices this spike in traffic, spins up a new copy of your Web server, and begins to load balance traffic across the (now three) web servers. As traffic continues to spike up, the AWS system repeats the process again and again until you have the correct number of Web servers for the traffic at the time. When the show is over and traffic to your website has begun to wane, the AWS system kicks into gear and automatically begins taking the last-created web server off-line, balancing traffic against the Web servers that are left. This process repeats itself as more and more people who watched the program leave your site. The big advantage here is that you do not have to size your environment for the worst-case scenario. (That is how we have wound up with data centers full of servers that are being utilized somewhere in the 2 to 10% range.) Instead, the AWS system spins up additional Web servers to meet the new traffic demand of the users who were watching the program. You are only charged for the use of each of the additional Web servers while they were active. As Web servers are taken off-line because there is not sufficient traffic to justify them, your charges for those servers cease immediately. You can architect the same solution for your application servers if they need that kind of scalability and a similar solution for your DB servers.

Does your internal architecture support this kind of elasticity? Sometimes moving to the Cloud isn't just about cost savings. Sometimes it's about the additional benefits you get from moving to the Cloud. In this particular case, it's really about both. Saving money with auto-scaling rather than over provisioning servers in case of higher-than-predicted demand also saves you money.

The Amazon IaaS offering is complete and provides a simple-to-use interface. You can get started with just a credit card. Many agencies are already doing simple projects on a credit card that once required a purchase order. Recently, AWS has made two significant announcements:

1. The availability of AWS GovCloud (US), a more secure offering that is directed at federal US government customers only. AWS GovCloud is currently hosted only in their western region but soon, the eastern region will be certified as well.

2. The award of the FISMA (Federal Information Security Management Act) Moderate Authorization and Accreditation from the US General Services Administration (GSA). With their other certifications (FISMA low, PCI DSS Level 1, FIPS 140-2, ISO 27001 and SAS-70 type II), they are a formidable environment for the government user.

Again, we will show you how to get started in depth with the AWS Cloud in the next chapter.

Before we move on, let me say a quick word about pricing. AWS understands they are infrastructure and thus need to be very competitive. That is why they have lowered prices 6 times in the last 4 years. The AWS IaaS Cloud is built on a multi-vendor solution, but the virtualization layer that they have chosen is Xen. This differs from some of the other vendors that we will examine. In contrast, the Terremark offering is built on VMware (who seems to have a resounding lead in the server virtualization industry). Does this give a vendor any advantage? What about when competition for IaaS Cloud services becomes keener as I predict it will over time? Perhaps it will give AWS a price advantage. As Jimmy Buffett says, "Only time will tell..."

Let's take a quick look at another IaaS offering that is a little different, but similar: Terremark.

The Terremark IaaS Offering

As stated earlier, Terremark's architecture is based on VMware® and their industry-leading vSphere virtualization technology. They have also implemented the VMware vCloud solution which will be discussed in chapter 16. (Terremark does have an offering called "vCloud Express", but they label it as only being suitable for "developmental teams and department needs.")

One immediate difference that you will notice with the Terremark Enterprise Cloud™ offering is that you cannot just give them a credit card and begin to use their service. You must order something first. Since one of the basic tenets of Cloud is that I can rapidly provision and de-provision machines to suit my needs, this is harder to do if I have to stop and place a purchase order first. What you order is a little different too. In the Terremark world, you order the amount of processing power you need, the amount of memory you need, plus the amount of disk space you need. Your total capacity equals whatever you can squeeze out of the environment that you have ordered.

There are a couple of things I really like about Terremark:

- Terremark is also a hosting company. Perhaps you don't want to virtualize your databases. Perhaps they are running on Solaris Sparc and you want to keep them that way. That's fine, but do you really want your web tier servers and your application tier servers, which we assume are virtualized, to be communicating with your database servers that are still sitting inside your firewalls? The usual answer is "of course not!" Normally, this would cause performance problems, although I am sure there are applications that write to a database once a week and are fine. But this is not best practice. All three tiers should reside in the same place. With Terremark, you can co-locate your existing database physical server with your virtual web and app servers and not be sending DB transactions across the WAN back to your data center.

- I like their Application Programming Interface (API). Because Terremark has implemented the vCloud API (more on this in chapter 16), they have implemented a whole set of API calls. It consists of a subset of standard VMware vCloud API calls as well as Terremark-specific API calls.

- Their interface is clean, simple, and works well.

Provisioning with Terremark differs slightly from AWS, but is still quite simple to do.

Once you place an order with Terremark or one of its resellers, they will email you a login. You then set up your password and add any other users you wish. Once you are signed in, you are presented with the Environment Resource Page. You immediately see the status of your resources (processor, memory and disk), devices (machines that you have created), and your network.

There is also a "Cloud Status" button which provides a quick snapshot of all of the datacenters for Terremark. There are three main US data centers based in Florida (Miami), California (Santa Clara) and Virginia (Culpeper), two of which are offered for their "Enterprise Cloud." Terremark is building other facilities but these are not yet in full production. Terremark also has two smaller data center facilities in South America and in Europe.

Terremark has been focusing on being "green." Their green initiatives are centered around two main areas:
1. Making the power and cooling of the IT equipment in their data center facilities as efficient as possible to reduce energy consumption
2. Virtualizing as much of the equipment and services as possible, so that the equipment can be shared and driven to much higher levels of efficiency. By making their equipment as efficient as possible, Terremark needs less of it, so they keep their power, cooling and space to a minimum, not to mention their prices.

To provision a server in the Terremark Enterprise Cloud, I first need to create a group name. Terremark uses the concept of "Rows" which is hierarchical level one for organizing servers. Within a Row are Server Groups, then come the servers. If I require many servers, this helps me organize them.

You can also import your current existing virtualized images. Since the OVF (Open Virtual Format) standard was just approved as an international standard by ISO and was previously approved by ANSI in 2010, it is now the standard for moving images from one virtualization (and Cloud) format to another. Although we will not discuss the import process, it is an important feature of the Terremark offering.

Now that I have created my group, I click the "Create Server" icon and start a wizard which will guide me the rest of the way.

It immediately asks me what kind of server I want to create (OS or OS and Database), using what operating system (Windows, Linux, Solaris), and what template. The system automatically generates a temporary root password for me (that you would change at the earliest opportunity), and provisions a 10 GB disk. Now I enter the server name and description along with the number of processors and the amount of RAM that I want for this system. Then I select the network options that I want for my new server. If I choose to put this server on the internal network a list of available IP addresses is presented to me. When I choose the IP address that I want, the subnet mask is filled in automatically. We are quickly and easily done with our wizard and are now presented with a summary screen containing all of the previous selections.

How do we add disks to our virtual machines? Again, very simply.

There are two ways to handle a Cloud monitoring feature in Terremark. Terremark has something called "burst mode." I can enable burst mode for both the processor and the memory in the environment. This is done at the environment level and not the individual machine level. If I enable it, I can exceed the processor and/or memory amounts that I have purchased if my virtual machines require it, but of course, I will be charged for it. This option is nice in that a pop up box shows up when I enable either one and informs me that I will be charged X per Y ($ per MHz or $ per GB) should burst mode be required.

Now that I have created my server, I will need to connect to that server via a Virtual Private Network (VPN). This is the only way to communicate with the servers! There are three things that you need to know about how VPNs work at Terremark:

- The VPN connection must be established and functioning properly in order to access any virtual servers. This includes Windows and Unix/Linux Servers.

- GRE Protocol 47, TCP Port 1723 and PPTP traffic must be allowed by your network for VPN connection to connect and function properly.
- The "Use Default Gateway of Remote Computer" option must be unchecked on both the IPv4 and IPv6 Advanced Properties of the VPN connection. (Windows)

In contrast to the CloudWatch feature of AWS, Terremark's resource bursting feature operates somewhat differently. Either option has saved the bacon of many an engineer, and for those of you with applications that need it, it is a true blessing for the Cloud user. Resource bursting allows an environment to expand on demand using a separately designated host resource pool, allowing your existing machines to use more resources, versus the AWS method of automatically cloning additional machines as demand requires it (and updating the load balancing), then deleting those machines and updating the corresponding load balancers (without kicking anyone off) as demand ebbs.

The Rackspace IaaS Offering

Rackspace® comes to Cloud from a hosting background, which they have kept in their current offerings.

They offer what they call a "Managed Hosting" environment where you can host virtualized and non-virtualized systems, as well as a Cloud Hosting environment. They also have a combination Managed-and-Cloud-Hosting environment, which is their hybrid offering.

Their Cloud environment has several notable features:

1. They use Xen® for their Linux virtual machines and XenServer® for their Windows virtual machines. It is all managed seamlessly through one interface.

2. They are also the only Cloud provider that I'm aware of at this time that has a management application developed for the iPhone™, iPad™ or iPod Touch™.

3. They have multiple Linux distributions, and Windows images (but no Solaris at this time).

4. All of their RAID storage is RAID-10 to provide additional protection during hardware failures.

5. All of their storage is persistent so if you turn off a virtual machine and turn it back on, all of your data will still be there

6. As of now, there is no import of OVF images as opposed to the others we have examined.

Rackspace has nine data centers throughout the world, including Texas (San Antonio (2), Dallas), Virginia (Herndon, Ashburn), and Illinois (Chicago) in the US. They also have facilities in the UK (London, Slough) and in Hong Kong.

An interesting feature of the Rackspace IaaS offering is that you can order directly from their web page and get started right way.

I did exactly that (figure 2-2) by clicking on the "More Information" button and was taken to the ordering page (figure 2-3).

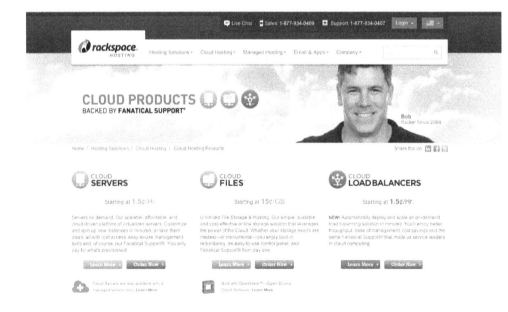

Figure 2-2: The Rackspace.com website. (© 2012 Rackspace US, Inc. Used under license)

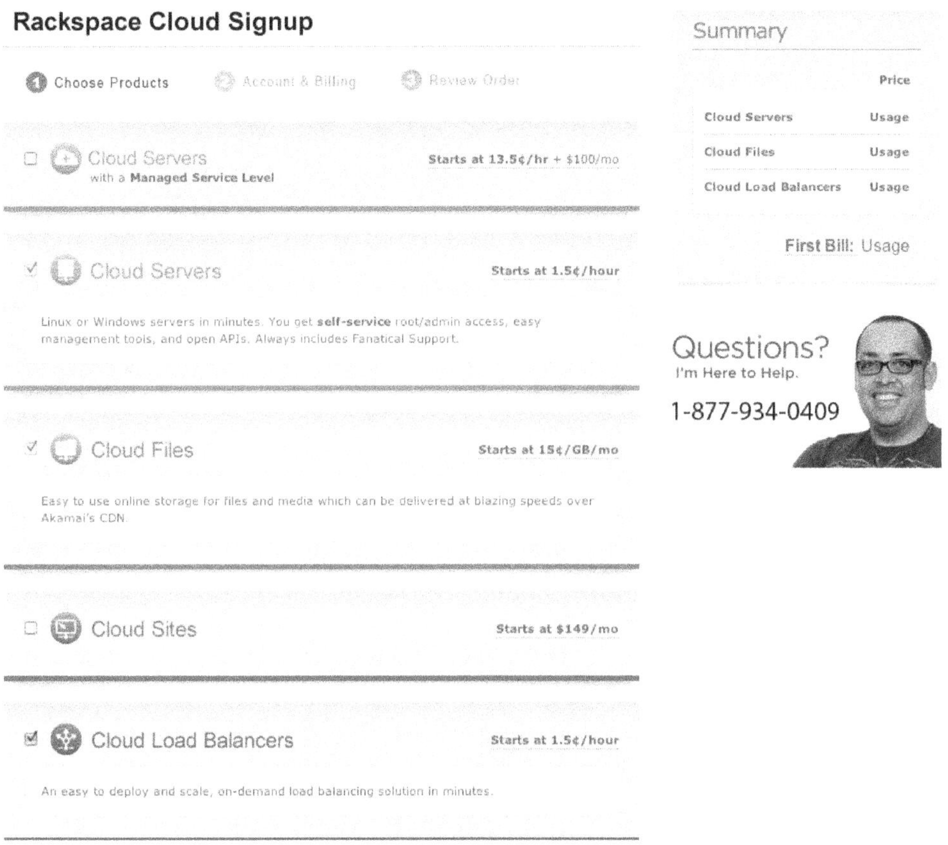

Rackspace Cloud Signup

1 Choose Products   2 Account & Billing   3 Review Order

	Price
Cloud Servers	Usage
Cloud Files	Usage
Cloud Load Balancers	Usage

☐ ⊕ Cloud Servers   Starts at 13.5¢/hr + $100/mo
with a **Managed Service Level**

First Bill: Usage

✓ Cloud Servers   Starts at 1.5¢/hour

Linux or Windows servers in minutes. You get **self-service** root/admin access, easy management tools, and open APIs. Always includes Fanatical Support.

Questions?
I'm Here to Help.

1-877-934-0409

✓ Cloud Files   Starts at 15¢/GB/mo

Easy to use online storage for files and media which can be delivered at blazing speeds over Akamai's CDN.

☐ Cloud Sites   Starts at $149/mo

☑ Cloud Load Balancers   Starts at 1.5¢/hour

An easy to deploy and scale, on-demand load balancing solution in minutes.

Figure 2-3: Rackspace Ordering page (© 2012 Rackspace US, Inc. Used under license)

As you can see, I ordered the Cloud Servers, Cloud Files (storage) and Cloud Load Balancers.

You sign up, create a username and password, give them your address, telephone and credit card information, and you are immediately online and ready to go. I was sent the customer welcome email asking me to create my secret question and answer should I forget my password. I was then presented with the main console page, shown in figure 2-4.

Again, what you get with Rackspace is a nice, easy-to-use website with a smooth provisioning process.

Figure 2-4: The Account Activity Screen (© 2012 Rackspace US, Inc. Used under license)

Summary

In this chapter, we have examined three IaaS Cloud providers: Amazon, Terremark and Rackspace. They all have pretty simple web interfaces, and while they all basically perform the same functions, each one does so slightly differently. Which one is right for you? That depends on your specific requirements. I like the security of the AWS GovCloud offering, as well as the number of special security certifications that they earned. But I like the simplicity of the Terremark site. For some workloads, basing their Cloud offering on VMware is a real plus. And I like Rackspace because I can get started with a simple-to-use interface. Plus, of the three providers we have discussed, Rackspace has the most data centers in the UK, as well as a data center in Hong Kong. But these are not the only providers serving these markets. There are strong native companies in both Europe and Asia. CloudSigma, a Zurich-based IaaS provider is ranked highly and, according to CloudTweaks.com, is in their top-25-to-watch list. Anise Asia is a privately owned company that is now servicing Malaysia, Indonesia and Thailand. In fact most of the major telecommunications carriers in Europe and Asia are either getting into the IaaS Cloud business or they are already there!

Amazon's credit card start-up method is quick and simple. Terremark's offering, however, can be a much more regular type of invoice. In this model, you purchase infrastructure hosted at the Terremark facility; the number of virtual machines you fit on the processor and memory that you bought is up to you. While this may be easier for the government to procure, and may work out fine in many cases, I can think of several examples where people have purchased a physical machine for a year, only to put two virtual machines on that physical box, which isn't any more efficient than what we have today.

Amazon offers the option to purchase their system in a similar but slightly conceptually different way. They're called fixed reserve instances. However, these differ in that they are fixed price instances that also accrue usage charges. While this does not necessarily help the purchasing process for the government, it does mean that you can save significant money over normal "on-demand" instances if you understand your usage patterns. There is even a chart on the AWS site to assist you in determining which type of EC2 instance will be the least expensive option for you.

All that being said, in reality, purchasing IaaS Cloud services is no more difficult than negotiating cell phone data plans that vary every month based on the number of users in the pool. Governments around the globe have been doing that for years!

3

Getting Started with AWS

AWS has a lot features...but how does it work? In itself, EC2 is very easy. You simply create a logon, setup a billing method which, for smaller users or proofs-of-concepts, is usually a credit card, and begin to request servers from the EC2. Amazon is the only IaaS Cloud vendor that allows you to start using the Cloud without prior contact with the company. Most of the other vendors require you to have some interaction with the company first and order something, then they will give you access to their management console. Not so with AWS. Simply create an account and give them a credit card to bill to and away you go! As you grow more sophisticated with Amazon, and your usage begins to exceed the monthly allowable credit card limits of your organization, you can set up purchase orders, checks, etc. But initially, you can start with a credit card.

Step 1: Creating an account

For our example, I've already created a new account, given AWS a credit card number, accepted the rules and regulations and have received my registration confirmation. Here is how that is done: make sure you go **http://aws.amazon.com**, because of course, http://www.amazon.com will take you to the parent company and world famous bookstore, Amazon.com. To create a login, simply click on the "Create an AWS Account" in the upper right-hand corner of the screen as shown in figure 3-1.

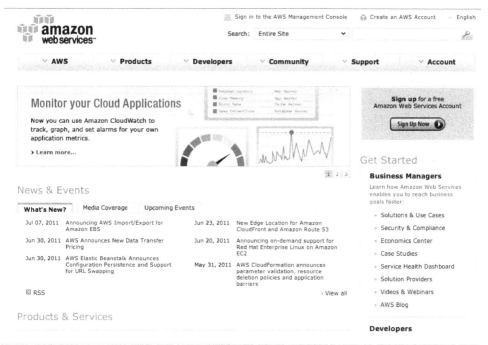

Figure 3-1 The Amazon Web Service home page
(©2012, Amazon Web Services LLC or its affiliates. All rights reserved.)

Once you create a login, accept the rules and regulations, and give them a credit card, you will get an email that looks like figure 3-2.

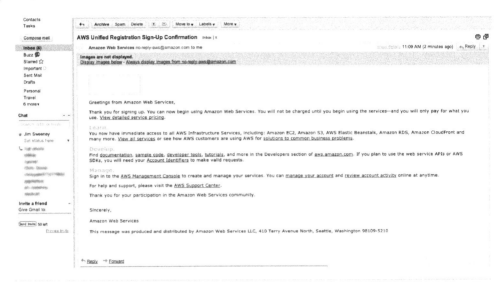

Figure 3-2: AWS Signup Confirmation

Step 2: Creating an EC2 instance

Now you are ready to log in and create an EC2 instance. Once you are logged in, (again, at **http://aws.amazon.com)**, simply click on the EC2 tab and click on the "Launch Instance" button as shown in figure 3-3.

Once you do that, you are taken through a wizard with several steps. I want to walk you through these steps because Amazon and the other IaaS providers have made it simple to get started.

Figure 3-3: Ready to launch an EC2 instance

Step 3: Launching your instance

In figure 3-4, we start the process. First, choose which kind of virtual machine (called an "instance" in AWS parlance) you wish to create. There are several Windows and Linux systems already created for you by default. You can also create one that you like and view it later it by clicking on the "My AMIs" tab. Or, you can click on the "Community AMIs" tab to see literally thousands of standard virtual machines of all types that have been already created and shared by other users.

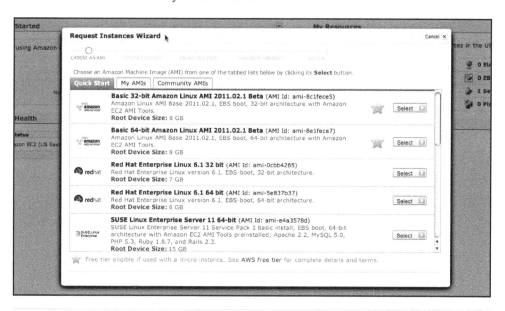

Figure 3-4: Requesting the EC2 Instance

Then specify where you want that virtual machine or instance to be created, how many instances you want to create, and the size of instance you want to create. There are several sizes of virtual machines. The smallest, for example, is a 1 core processor with 1GB RAM and the largest (at least at this time) is 8 cores with 68 GB of RAM. AWS has named all of their sizes for easy reference and, in our example, I have selected here the "High-Memory, Double-Extra-Large" instance, as you can see in figure 3-5.

At this point, you are ready to add "tags" to your virtual machines

Figure 3-5: Selecting the instance details

or instance. Tags are metadata for your instances. Each EC2 tag consists of a key and a value, both of which you define. You could define a set of tags for your instances to help you track each instance's owner and OSI model stack level. For example, I could

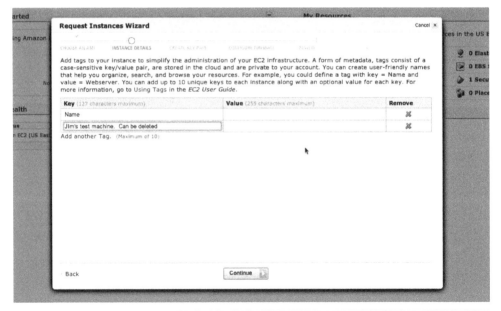

Figure 3-6: Instances and Tags

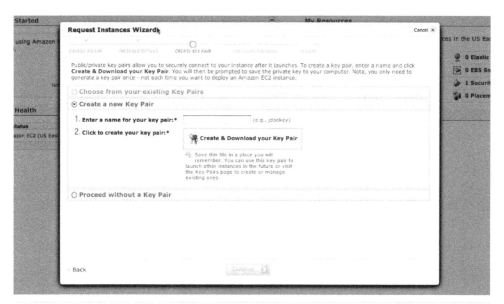

Figure 3-7: Key Pair creation

assign two tags to each of your instances, one called "*Owner*" and another called "*Stack*". Each of the tags also has an associated value, perhaps "Jim Sweeney" and "TestDB." These are used to help you search and manage all of your instances in whatever manner best suits your environment. In figure 3-6, the screenshot shows where to enter these tags for your newly created instance.

At this point, if you have not created a "key pair," you will need to do so. Key pairs are used to securely connect to your instance once it is created. If you have already created a key pair, there is no need to do so again. Simply enter the name of the key pair and you are ready to begin. Combined with the firewall, which will be seen in the next illustration, they establish a secure environment that only you can reach. See figure 3-7 for the key pair creation wizard.

To create the security groups for your instance, the wizard will guide you through this process (figure 3-8). Firewall rules can be as simple – or as complicated – as necessary to get the job done without getting in your way. Each instance can belong to its own security group, or many instances can belong to the same security group. For example, you could say that only a certain set of

Figure 3-8: Security Groups and Firewall rules
(©2012, Amazon Web Services LLC or its affiliates. All rights reserved.)

IP addresses can connect to the database server using the SSH (for you to control the instance), and other than that, the only IP addresses that can connect to the DB server are those from your app servers and they (the app servers) can only connect on one certain port. Period. No one else gets through. They are just like the firewalls at your internal facility, only easier to manage, and, one could argue, a lot more secure! Are your firewall rules set up to only let the servers that need to talk to each other do so? Figure 3-8 shows the security group creation process. This is one of the many features that can make Cloud more secure than your data center.

Finally, we come to the end of the wizard and the summary screen. As you can see from figure 3-9, there are a couple of things that I did not mention during the instance creation process. Things like: What to do when you power off the instance? Should the AWS system delete it? Or should it power off, but keep it available for you? What about protection from accidental deletion of your instance? This is a true/false feature that is enabled or disabled in the creation process. There are a few others but the basics are exactly the same.

Figure 3-9: The Instance Creation Summary screen
(©2012, Amazon Web Services LLC or its affiliates. All rights reserved.)

Also in figure 3-9, you will see something called "Instance Class" with the value for the instance we created labeled "On Demand." This is the norm. You start it up when you need it, or "on demand," and shut it down when you no longer need it. And, remember, you only pay for it when you are actually using it.

There is another option for Instance Class called "Spot Price." To my knowledge, Amazon is the only one that is currently offering such a feature. Here's how it works. Let's say that you have an application that requires that you process a database. You believe that it will take some time to run. Let's also assume that you really don't have an approaching deadline for this project. It needs to get done, but it's not critical that it be completed tomorrow or even the next day. You could employ "Spot Instances" to process your database. Spot Instances let you pay for computer capacity by the hour at a "Spot Price" that fluctuates based on supply and demand. You specify a maximum rate you are willing to pay per hour, and your instance only runs when the Spot Price is at or below that price. When you are running computer tasks with flexible start and end times, you can save money by running your workload at an off time at a reduced cost. Or you could use Spot instances another way. Since it is a rare occurrence when Spot Prices are greater than on-demand, you could use on-demand instances for your core systems and Spot Instances for your compute nodes in a large data analysis job for example. Remember, though, that if the Spot Price suddenly climbs above the price you are willing to pay, your Spot Instances will be terminated! This is important, so while Spot Instances can save you money, you need to have the right situation to use them for maximum effectiveness.

You may wonder why the price fluctuates. This may seem a bit odd, but there are a couple of factors that determine the price:

- The time of day and the day of the week/month. Most workloads are heaviest from 8 a.m. to 5 p.m., regardless of the time zone. At other times, the AWS system has less to do, so in return for being flexible, you get a discounted price.
- Amazon is currently (at least at this time) adding enough infrastructure (servers, storage, etc) to their current Cloud every day to support a business equal to the size of their world-wide Amazon.com bookstore in 2004. Needless to say, that's a lot of capacity! When you are growing as fast as they are, there are bound to be times when they have a little capacity left over! If you have the right type of workload, you can take advantage of it.

That's it. Hit launch and away you go. From start up to launch, it only takes a few minutes to get started.

Incidentally, you can use a DHCP IP address for your instance or you can request a pool of static IP addresses that you control and mete out to your instances. Once these addresses are assigned to your account, they are yours until you decide you no longer need them and decide to turn them back in. One word of caution: you will be charged for all of the addresses you request, whether you use them or not. This prevents people from hoarding IP addresses, and it certainly seems like a fair way to do it for everyone.

"What about storage?" you ask. "This is great for servers, but how do we handle storage?" In the AWS system there are a couple of kinds of storage. For now, we'll focus on the storage you would use with an EC2 instance, called EBS, or Elastic Block Storage. It used to be that storage associated with EC2 instances was not persistent but that changed a while ago. Now, every time you power off an EC2 instance (virtual machine), you do not reset the EBS storage to the default for that image. So if you create a machine and store a number of files on it, when you power off that machine, those additional files will be still be there. It's a good idea to create some storage on which you can securely keep your files. Think of this as your "C:" drive being the place for the OS, but not stored data, and your "D:" drive as the shared storage on which you store all of your programs, data, etc.

Step 4: Creating block storage

Figure 3-10 shows you the start of the wizard that you use to create EC2 block storage. Block storage is defined as network-attached storage as opposed to a storage area network. It is important to remember that **all storage within the EC2 system is block storage.** Within the AWS system, there is no such thing as fiber channel storage. As you can see in figure 3-10, I have selected the "volumes" under the Elastic Block Storage heading.

Figure 3-10: Creating an EC2 Volume
(©2012, Amazon Web Services LLC or its affiliates. All rights reserved.)

The other thing you can do under this heading is manage snapshots. You can take snapshots of your volumes and manage them like any other. For disaster protection, you could take a snapshot of a volume and then move that snapshot to another region or zone. (Note: there are no volumes shown in figure 3-10.)

Create Volume   Cancel ✕

        Size: 1   [TiB ⬍]

Availability Zone: [us-east-1b ⬍]

    Snapshot: [--- No Snapshot --- ⬍]

❌ Volume of 2048GiB is too large; maximum is 1024GiB.

                                    [Cancel] [Yes, Create]

Figure 3-11: Creating a volume

As soon as you click on the volumes button a new screen pops up, as shown in figure 3-11.

As you can see from figure 3-11, I attempted to create a volume that was bigger than 1 TB. The AWS system gave me an error, so I reduced the size of the volume that I wanted to create to 1 TB. Now I hit the "yes, create" button, and we see the results in figure 3-12. As you can see in figure 3-12, our volume has been created. In

Figure 3-12: Results of our Volume Creation

this screen, you will see all of your volumes, when they were created, what zone they are in, and their current status. I could have created a volume that already had a snapshot attached to it. For example, suppose I created a Windows 2008 R2 instance and then I decided that I needed to install additional software from the Windows 2008 R2 disc. When I created my volume, I simply would have indicated the snapshot that I wanted to create the volume from, instead of the "No snapshot" option that I chose (figure 3-11). You could infer from this that you could take regular snapshots of all of your volumes, move those snapshots to another zone, and create new EC2 instances with those snapshots in record time. And of course, you would be right. Also, you will be charged for Elastic Block Storage (EBS) volumes based on the size of the volume, not how much of the volume is in use at the moment. So be careful that you don't create 1 TB volumes when in reality, you only need a volume that is a couple of hundred GB.

Figure 3-13 shows the dashboard that monitors your entire EC2 environment. As you can see, I currently have no running instances, no EBS volumes, and no IP addresses because – since I created these solely as part of the demo for this chapter – I deleted them immediately, since I had no use for them and didn't want to pay for them.

Figure 3-13: The EC2 Dashboard
(©2012, Amazon Web Services LLC or its affiliates. All rights reserved.)

Figure 3-14: Starting EC2 instances with CloudWatch

Step 5: Invoking CloudWatch

Invoking CloudWatch is very simple and can be done when you create an instance. As you can see in figure 3-14, the process starts normally.

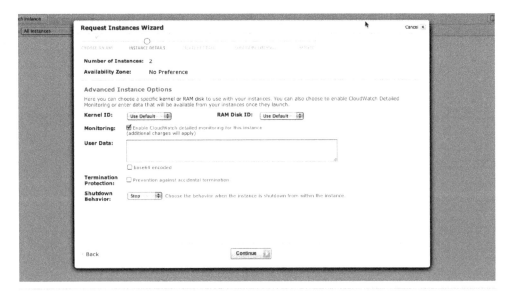

Figure 3-15: Enabling Monitoring

Figure 3-16: Instances with CloudWatch

On the next screen of the wizard, all you have to do is check an additional box, called Monitoring, as shown in figure 3-15.

Note that in figure 3-16, I chose the smallest instance possible. Web servers can be very small when they are processing mostly network traffic.

I have created my small instances and started them up. When I click on the CloudWatch tab above, let's look at what CloudWatch can do (figure 3-17).

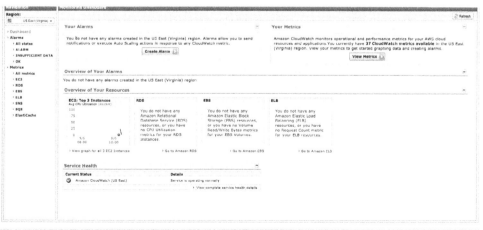

Figure 3 17: CloudWatch

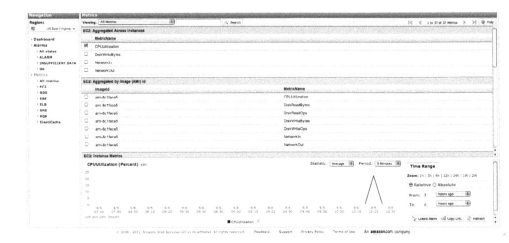

Figure 3-18: CloudWatch Metrics
(©2012, Amazon Web Services LLC or its affiliates. All rights reserved.)

CloudWatch is now active and monitoring my instances. You do pay for the CloudWatch service, but I would rather enable it when my traffic has the potential to be volatile, as with many web servers today. As you can also see in the example, I could also enable CloudWatch for RDS, EBS and ELB (Elastic Load Balancers). Before we leave the CloudWatch introduction, let's take a quick look at some of the many metrics that are available (figure 3-18).

Click on any of the metrics and you will instantly see how the monitored items, in this case my EC2 instances, are performing. As you can see above, I activated CPU Utilization. When I started them up, I observe a peak of approximately 25%; they have since dropped down to near zero which is perfectly logical as I do not yet have traffic flowing across them.

Step 6: Creating Load Balancers

Enabling the load balancing features is done through the EC2 console. By clicking on the Load Balancers Navigation button on the left, in figure 3-19, you will see that I have not yet created a Load Balancer.

Figure 3-19: Elastic Load Balancers

Click on the "Create Load Balancer" button (there are actually a couple to choose from, but they get you to the same place). The wizard will present you with the screen shown in figure 3-20. For illustration purposes, I have created a very basic load balancer. I am taking port 80 requests, which we know is the default port for web traffic. I am going to load balance the traffic and spit out requests, again on port 80, to my two EC2 instances.

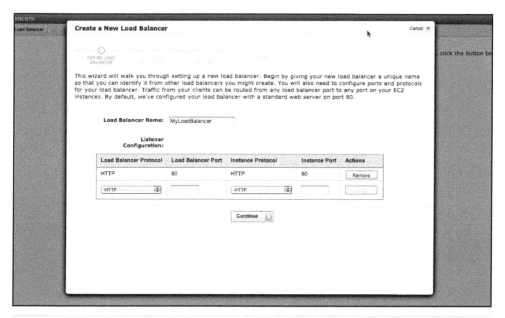

Figure 3-20: Load Balancer Creation Wizard

In reality, this is not a very secure way to do things, and is not considered best practice, but for the sake of this example, I have chosen this configuration.

In figure 3-21, I set various configuration options, including advanced options, which indicate how long to wait for the health check ping before AWS declares an EC2 instance dead and no longer sends traffic to it, among others.

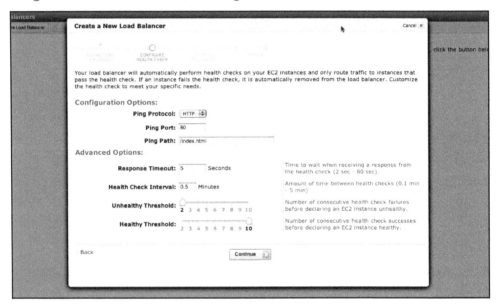

Figure 3-21: Creating the Load Balancer

Now I choose the EC2 instances across which this load balancer is going to balance traffic. In figure 3-22, I have selected the two instances that I created previously. Note that you do not have to load balance across just these two. There could be three or more, but especially with the CloudWatch feature enabled, starting with a small number like two or three seems to make sense for most customers.

In figure 3-23, I can review my choices, and make sure I am satisfied with everything before hitting the "create" button

Figure 3-22: Selecting the EC2 instances

and creating the load balancer. I return to the Load Balancers
Navigation screen (figure 3-24) and I can see my load balancer
and all of the various details about it.

Figure 3-23: ELB Creation - Summary Screen

It's really that easy to set up a couple of web servers, enable load balancing of the web traffic across them, and enable CloudWatch to create additional web servers when and if it becomes necessary to do so.

IaaS Case Study 1

Jet Propulsion Laboratory (JPL)

The Agency:
NASA Jet Propulsion Lab

Their Challenge:
Find creative and inexpensive ways to use new technology to make their budget go farther

Their Solution:
Start using Cloud for small projects and now use Cloud for all new missions

The NASA Jet Propulsion Lab (JPL) may be most famous for the recent Mars rover program that brought back exciting images from Mars using two rovers, named "Opportunity," and "Spirit." These two rovers were launched in 2003 to land on Mars and begin traversing the Red Planet in search of signs of past life.

Or maybe Cassini-Huygens comes to mind when you think of JPL. It is currently orbiting the ringed planet Saturn and its numerous moons. The Cassini spacecraft has been – and continues to be – a keystone of exploration of the Saturnian system and the properties of gaseous planets in our solar system.[6]

Fans of the movie "Star Trek: The Motion Picture," may even remember the Voyager series as one of JPL's projects. In the movie, Voyager 6 returns as V'ger, a probe which has gathered so much data it achieved consciousness.

But did you know that there are currently 36 active missions being operated out of JPL? That shouldn't astonish anyone – trailblazing has been JPL's charter since it was established by the California Institute of Technology in the 1930s. Even America's first satellite, Explorer 1, launched in 1958, was created at JPL. As NASA Kennedy Space Center and NASA Johnson Space Center are to the US manned space program, so JPL is to unmanned missions.

NASA is ahead of the technology curve in many respects. They are big users of the Amazon Web Services (AWS) Cloud, as well as many other Cloud providers. Here are a few of the many ways that JPL is using the Cloud:

- When "Opportunity" and "Spirit" were launched, no one anticipated that they would still be going 6 years later. In fact, John Talis, Program Manager for the Mars Rover program, projected the original mission would last 90 days. Therefore the infrastructure that was purchased for that mission contained only enough storage to accommodate 90 days worth of data. When

---

6 JPL Web site at www.jpl.nasa.gov

these rovers outperformed their initial design constraints, what should be the solution? Throw away that data? Certainly not! As the Microsoft commercial goes: "To the Cloud." Note: "Spirit" ceased to function on March 22, 2010, 6 years after the rover landed on Mars, but "Opportunity" is still going strong!

- JPL used the AWS Cloud during its annual testing of their ATHLETE (All-Terrain Hex-Limbed Extra-Terrestrial) robot. This robot was developed as a multi-purpose vehicle to travel across a variety of terrains, from smooth and flat to rolling hills and even on steep mountainous terrain. As part of the D-RATS (Desert Research and Training Studies), every year JPL takes the ATHLETE robot to the desert and tests the performance of ATHLETE against other NASA robots. Operators rely on high-resolution satellite images for remote guidance, positioning and situational awareness during these tests. These images are all stored and processed on a modular workflow auto-mation framework called Polyphony, which streamlines the process by leveraging hundreds of individual instances in the AWS Cloud.
- As part of the Cassini project, JPL stores over 180,000 images from Saturn in the AWS Cloud.

NASA has a long history of Cloud use, but they didn't start out with mission data, that's for sure. I was fortunate to interview Tomas Soderstrom, CTO for IT for NASA JPL, who gave me a brief history of the use of Cloud at JPL.

"The reason that we got interested in Cloud in the first place was that Cloud was one of seven technologies that we identified as a potential game changer," said Mr. Soderstrom. "We formed a Cloud Working Group made up of IT and non-IT people at NASA JPL. We found that people in our organization were already using Cloud and hiding it from IT. We figured that we needed a coor-dinated effort to investigate Cloud and see what we could use it for at JPL without hiding it from the IT security police! We went to these folks and told them that they did not have to hide. In fact, we would fund their efforts. We wanted to see how we could take advantage of Cloud at JPL."

JPL figured, if they did not embrace it, users would bypass IT and use the Cloud anyway. If users did go around and things blew up, the IT department would still get the blame. It's like the law – ignorance of the law does not make you innocent. Ignoring those already using the Cloud would not shift the blame away from the IT department in the event of a catastrophe. Khawaja Shams was the Leader of the Cloud Working Group. He had a vested interest in the use of Cloud at JPL. He was also one of the software engineers for the team that developed the software for the Mars rovers.

"We put public, private and even semi-private data in the Cloud," said Tomas. "The important difference is that we looked at Cloud as a science experiment and not an IT experiment. One thing we were afraid of was vendor lock-in. By trying several Cloud platforms, we discovered that different platforms are good for different things."

The first thing that they did was to classify all of their data into a "Wheel of Security". By putting the different types of data into a spreadsheet and classifying them according to security level, they were able to create a pie chart showing data ranging from low levels of security classification, to slightly higher security, to the highest levels of security classification. They started with the lowest level data, which were the pictures of Mars.

In cooperation with Microsoft, and using the Microsoft Windows Azure Cloud (which we will discuss in Chapters 10 and 14) they developed an online game called "Be A Martian"[7] which is still up and running today. "The important thing is that this allowed us to design a game that needed some of the unique features of Cloud, including the ability to scale up and down as needed," said Tom. "It also garnered us lots of media attention for our use of the Cloud."

7 Beamartian.jpl.nasa.gov

After these successes, NASA JPL decided to try an outreach approach where they put public images of Mars in the AWS Cloud and participants wrote code to control Lego™ robots. The robots that were able to pick up the most rocks with their robots were the winners. The code was so well written and performed so well that NASA actually took this code and used some of it in the code that controls the real live Mars rovers!

Soderstrom observed, "Because this project didn't go into the traditional IT queue, it didn't take us months to develop it. So that led us to thinking...Could we use the Cloud in a real mission?" They had 180,000 images of Saturn from the Cassini project. But they had a problem processing them. Because they only had a single server, they were taking 15 days running 24/7 in their lab to process the images. By spinning up a bunch of AWS servers, or instances, the total processing took less than 5 hours and cost JPL less than $200. "This was the epiphany," said Tom. "Everything really took off from there as far as our use of the Cloud. We then went on to write CASM – The Cloud Application Suitability Model. This is a series of questions for developers to help them determine which Cloud is best for their particular application. It turns out that we discovered we really want to write software for our various projects, like controlling robots in space, not run our own infrastructure."

Then came the ATHLETE robot. Because of the processing time for the images necessary to remotely pilot the robot, and the limited processing power at NASA JPL, the engineers were only able to run approximately 1 test per day. Once they switched to the AWS Cloud, they were immediately able to process images much more quickly and inexpensively, allowing them to run 5 simulations per day in the Arizona desert. This ultimately saved the program, and taxpayers, money. Remember, when the once-yearly test was done, the servers that processed those images were not needed until next year, so JPL released them back to the AWS Cloud for someone else to use and, more importantly, stopped paying for them. This saved even more money for the program and US taxpayers. As Tom told me, "We saved an order of magnitude on the cost and we gained a 2x order of magnitude on the response time of the system by using AWS. We can take advantage of their massive scale to encrypt and decrypt images."

Although JPL started with one configuration in the AWS Cloud, they quickly switched to another. In the AWS Cloud, you can set up things so that the virtual instances are treated as part of your virtual data center. No one else can access those instances or the storage associated with them. This is called a Virtual Private Cloud or VPC. "We used to use AWS as a Virtual Private Cloud, but after this project, we believed the security was good enough that we dropped that extra layer of security and just stored en-crypted images in the public AWS Cloud."

Tom actually agrees with many others in the industry now, includ-ing Ira (Gus) Hunt, who is the CTO for the CIO at the CIA, and me. We believe that Cloud is more secure than what you are currently doing in-house, for three main reasons:

1. The massive scale makes the probability that someone hack-ing into the Cloud and finding enough of your particular data to make sense out of it is minimal.

2. There are additional security measures that one can take in the Cloud like encryption of data at rest and data in transit, etc.

3. Because data centers have different equipment of different ages with different versions of operating systems, it makes the task of keeping them all patched to the latest revisions difficult. With the Cloud, everything is new and everything from the virtualization layer down is kept patched by the Cloud vendor. All you need to worry about is the OS and application stacks.

Of course, for more secure workloads, Tomas recommends the VPC architecture. And he believes in the new FedRAMP initiative. "FedRAMP, if successful, will supersede us. It will really make acquisition of the Cloud much easier. I really applaud what they are trying to do."

The consolidated billing from AWS gives JPL the advantage of buying as one agency, but allows the programs that use the Cloud to manage their own Cloud resources individually. Tom continued, "This has really made purchasing easier for us. Other Cloud vendors do this well too, but it seems like AWS does it particularly well."

Tom recently spoke at an RSA security conference on Cloud computing. "I thought I was going to stand up there and get creamed by everyone from a security perspective, but I didn't. I told them that Cloud is The Force and you are Luke Skywalker. You can either embrace it or you can be destroyed by it!"

According to Tom, they quickly learned three important lessons about the Cloud:

- Start with a "Wheel of Security" and start testing. Test with public data and learn from it. The Cloud operates very differently, even vendors operate differently, and it is a learning experience.

- License agreements are sometimes difficult to negotiate. Tom said, "We spent a lot of time educating ourselves and our users on the different vendors, how they work and how they license. It took us a while and was not easy to get started."

- JPL used a cross-functional team to assess the use of Cloud. Because Cloud is different, the billing is different and that sometimes takes a while to understand.

Now JPL uses Cloud for everything. All missions are using the Cloud in one way or another. "Our goal," says Soderstrom, "is to never buy another server again. Period." This has also changed his thinking around IT. As he says: "The interesting thing is that IT as we know it is dying. The new model is IT and the business or agency end-user coming together to innovate. If IT gets it, they can enable the mission of the business in a much more agile, and cost-effective manner."

Tom credits Jim Rinaldi, CIO at JPL, and his leadership for JPL's fast start in Cloud. "He really built a partnership between the IT department and the mission engineers. He was really instrumental in our transition to the Cloud."

JPL is leading the way in the government's use of Cloud to save money and time, while providing better and faster services to their customers and the general public. This agency is continually innovating and this case study shows they are greatly reaping the benefits of doing so.

IaaS Case Study 2
USA.gov

The agency:
The United States Government

Their challenge:
Creating a flexible web portal capable of expanding and contracting with user traffic

Their solution:
Using the Terremark Cloud as needed to provide additional capacity on demand

When you need important information about the United States Government and its services, the best place to go is **USA.gov**, the official web portal and information source for the federal government. The primary goal of the website is to give the public an easy, efficient way to interact with the government.

USA.gov and its Spanish-language companion site, GobiernoUSA. gov, are repositories of information about local, state, and federal government. Users can obtain information about a wide variety of government services: grant instructions, consumer guides, health and nutrition updates, tax forms, driver's license renewal, and voter registration information. A very popular site, on any given day the site receives approximately 100 million visits.

This web site also serves as a hub for dissemination of critical information, so traffic increases substantially in times of crisis when critical data is released and/or data must be accessed by many people. Two commonly-encountered examples are: when unemployment statistics are released or when natural disasters occur. In the past, when events such as these took place, users suffered long delays or crashed sites as a result of too much site traffic.

Normally the General Services Administration (GSA) would procure additional servers, storage and network equipment to handle heavy traffic spikes. But when that infrastructure wasn't needed, those resources would sit idle, using power and cooling, and of course, taking up unnecessary space in the data center. They would also be depreciating, requiring funds to maintain software and operating systems licenses, as well as maintenance contracts. Clearly, GSA needed a way to improve service, but they had some very specific requirements that not everyone could meet. Their new security regulations included multifactor authentication, resource tracking, packet flow analysis, PCI compliance, the Health Insurance Portability and Accountability Act (HIPAA) compliance, and significant on-site data center security.

The solution? GSA would host most of the infrastructure

necessary to handle normal traffic volumes in their own data center, but would use Terremark as a "hot-standby" site. This arrangement allowed them to contract for a minimal amount of computing power which could be rapidly and automatically expanded when site traffic spiked. This was a smart decision on many levels. First, GSA opted for Terremark's self-service, portal-based Cloud service that we examined in Chapter 1. In this Infrastructure-as-a-Service (IaaS) platform, USA.gov has a minimum baseline capacity on a 12-month contract. When they need burst capability to provide additional resources, however, it is automatically there. This keeps their costs at a minimum, but provides them the automatic capacity ups and downs required by the user community. Users would no longer be frustrated with slow response times or get kicked off a system that could not handle the volume of traffic thrown its way. When traffic is at normal levels, GSA pays only the contracted baseline fee; when traffic spikes they can accommodate large volumes of traffic and pay for the capacity they use. Because GSA never knows exactly what kind of capacity it will need, it made perfect sense to move to a Cloud platform with this capability.[8]

The Terremark Cloud offered benefits, too. USA.gov wanted a system that would require a minimal amount of time for migration. USA.gov required a very short testing process. Because the original site had previously been deployed in-house on Egenera BladeFrame systems and VMware, which stored workloads in virtual machines, it was easy to copy the virtual machines (which we know are just files) to Terremark's VM-based Cloud platform, which also runs VMware. The actual migration took only 10 days, while the test validation occurred over the course of a single weekend.

Addressing GSA's additional security requirements, Terremark designed its multitenant environment to meet the rigorous security monitoring and transparency demands of customers like government agencies. With only a few minor adjustments in

8 From the Terremark Case study: http://www.terremark.com/uploadedFiles/Industry_Solutions/Federal_Government/Case%20Study-%20USA.gov%20Achieves%20Cloud%20Bursting%20Efficiency%20Using%20Terremark's%20Enterprise%20Cloud.pdf, 2009.

policy, GSA was able to get the monitoring and reporting it needed for the USA.gov website. In addition to these adjustments, GSA also added a number of its own security elements on top of the Terremark Cloud environment. GSA required multifactor authentication (MFA) to access the USA.gov administrative portal, along with the ability to track various resources so that they would know exactly where each piece of data resided. They also wanted 128-bit encryption for traffic and the ability to conduct their own packet flow analysis to ensure that what they thought was being transmitted was really the only thing being transmitted between the GSA and Terremark sites!

The site is hosted out of Terremark's Culpeper, Virginia facility. Not only have they been certified for FISMA moderate workloads, but they have also been audited against the NIST 800-53 standards. From a physical security perspective, some measures that Terremark have taken include: 250 motion sensor cameras, Department of Defense-approved fences, and blast-proof exteriors.

In a Terremark press release, Martha Dorris, GSA's Deputy Associate Administrator of The Office of Citizen Services, estimated that the move to Terremark's Cloud platform will cut costs by 90%, while improving capabilities with the newfound infrastructure flexibility.[9]

During a news conference at NASA's Ames Research Center on September 15, 2009, former federal government CIO Vivek Kundra discussed the GSA's ability to reduce costs while adding flexibility for the federal government's official website, USA.gov. "The selection of Terremark's Enterprise Cloud to power USA.gov resulted in a reduction of annual costs from $2.5 million to $800,000, as well as providing the scalability to dynamically provision Cloud computing resources within minutes instead of weeks. In addition, the agile computing infrastructure allows GSA to deploy upgrades to

9 ibid

USA.gov in 24 hours instead of the 6 months typically required in a traditional model."[10]

At this point, you may be thinking, "This isn't really a Cloud at all. This is just using a Cloud provider as overflow capacity." A Government Computing News (GCN) blog entry from 2009 entitled, "But is it Really Cloud Computing?"[11] asked the same question. Here are some excerpts from that blog:

...The agency appears ahead of the curve...Except, the service GSA is using may not actually be, strictly speaking, Cloud computing...Two of the key attributes are "rapid elasticity" and "pay per use."

The offering, called Enterprise Cloud (E-Cloud) does not exactly fit the profile of Cloud computing, though it is definitely a step away from the hosting services that many of the company's competitors offer. With most hosting services, you can contract space out on a server, using the operating system provided.

With Terremark, you supply a VMware-based image of your complete operating environment, including an operating system (either from you or provided by the company)...So, we presume that is what GSA is doing is moving the entire array of USA.gov sites, along with the supporting content management system, into a VMware instance, where it will be run on Terremark's servers.

Like traditional hosting services, Terremark bills on a monthly basis. Users estimate how much processing power they need and use the estimates to pick the most appropriate plan. If their usage goes over these limits, customers pay an overage, but, like cell phone users, they can switch to a larger plan in the following months.

No discounts are offered for not using less than the full capacity, though. And this is strikingly different from Cloud services from Google and Amazon, both of which charge only for the actual CPU, storage and bandwidth that was used.

So, is what GSA is using actually Cloud computing? Or is it a

10 Vivek Kundra Press Conference, September 15, 2009
11 http://gcn.com/Blogs/Tech-Blog/2009/05/GSA-Cloudy.aspx

slightly different sort of hosting model, an admittedly innovative one based on virtualization?

On the one hand, it does not have the truly elastic pricing that Amazon does, where you literally can buy 47 cents worth of computing if you need to. But it does allow the user to scale up and down as traffic waxes and wanes, admittedly on a month-to-month basis.

As federal agencies move into this exciting new world of out-sourcing, they may have to answer such thorny questions (GSA itself certainly seems to be grappling with the issue). Or, better yet, maybe they won't worry so much about getting in compli-ance with the latest buzzword.

Remember that this blog post was written in 2009, and USA.gov is quite possibly the very first instance of the federal government attempting to operate in the Cloud. While I would like to see them move everything to the Cloud, using multiple data centers and taking advantage of bursting capability at both sites to further reduce costs associated with having their own servers, storage, licenses, maintenance, etc., this shows that the federal govern-ment is making strides toward moving to the Cloud. In our next example, which took place two years later, we will see how a gov-ernment customer successfully moved everything to the Cloud.

The blogger had a problem with the pricing model of Terremark. I disagree. On the AWS website, you will see something called "Reserved Instances." You buy these up front for the year and you pay for them, whether you use them or not. You also pay for usage, but in theory the combo is less expensive if you know your workload requirements. After some period of time, we all know approximately what our traffic will be on a normal day-to-day basis. Amazon prices this as an option for their customers. In the Terremark model, this is just the way of life. And since you can, in fact, burst up and back down to that monthly committed number, you do have the rapid elasticity of Cloud according to NIST.

In June 2009, The Web100 named USA.gov as Number 50 on its "Top 100 websites." They ranked above AOL, MSNBC, and 48 others. Also in June 2009, the Brookings Institution named USA. gov as the Number 1 federal web site.[12]

GSA's USA.gov is one of the very first initiatives that the federal government took toward moving to the Cloud. As we will see in the coming chapters and case studies, in the three years since USA.gov moved, things have come a long, long way!

12 From USA.gov's website at http://www.usa.gov/About/Awards.shtml

6

Software as a Service Clouds (SaaS) for Email and Collaboration

Software-as-a-Service Clouds are very simple. You use the software that you need when you need it and you only pay for it when you use it. When you are done using the software, you are also done paying for its use. With a SaaS Cloud you do not own the software that you are using. You do not pay for the software license, the hardware on which to run it, or the electricity to power and cool that server. In addition, you do not need to patch the OS or the software itself, upgrade to new versions, or back up your application or your data. This is all handled automatically. Back to our basic chart for a look at how the SaaS model differs from other Cloud delivery models.

Figure 6-1: The SaaS Model

As you can see from figure 6-1, the only interface that the user has with a SaaS model is with the software itself. The user does not need to worry about the network, server hardware, storage, hypervisor, guest operating system or even the middleware that the software needs to do its job. The underlying infrastructure, the physical security, power, cooling, space, hardware and software maintenance all become the responsibility of the SaaS provider. Of course, some SaaS providers believe that they are good at software development but not handling all of the infrastructure stuff so they host their application on top of a traditional IaaS Cloud. This further complicates the issue but in this scenario each participant is doing what they do best:

- **IaaS provider** – Infrastructure, physical security, maintenance, power, cooling, etc

- **SaaS provider** – The software and middleware/databases needed for the software, the patching/ upgrading of the software, and the backup/disaster recovery procedures necessary to maintain the SLAs

- **The User/Buyer** – They concentrate on what they do best, whether it is securing the homeland, or protecting and serving, or overseeing America's nuclear reactors. Whatever the mission of your organization is, you are now free to concentrate on it. In this scenario you do not have to detract any energy from your mission because that is now someone else's job.

Because at its core, it is a very simple model to understand, many organizations are already using SaaS services. The most popular applications that are used in a SaaS delivery model are:

- Customer relationship management (CRM)
- Marketing automation
- Customer service and support
- Enterprise resource planning (ERP)
- Accounting and expense management
- Human resource management
- Travel booking
- Supply chain management (SCM) sourcing, procurement
- Warehouse management
- Content, communication, and collaboration (CCC) web conferencing
- E-mail and collaboration
- E-learning

Some very popular CRM/ERP applications include Salesforce.com, Oracle® on SaaS, and SAP® on SaaS. But there are numerous small/niche players in the field too. There are a few I really like: HyperOffice®, which is a collaboration suite in the Cloud, and Sonian®, which handles email archiving and e-discovery in the Cloud.

Let me just touch very quickly on HyperOffice. HyperOffice is an integrated collaboration, messaging and mobility technology delivered through the Cloud.

The core components of HyperOffice include:

Business class email and messaging – with all the features of a business class email system, archiving, search, drag-and-drop Ajax interface, support for all browsers, mobile devices, POP and IMAP.

Core Collaboration – contacts, calendars, document management, project management, wikis, intranets and extranets, forums and voting.

Mobility – push email and wireless synching of contacts, calendars, projects and notes out to iPhone®, Android®, BlackBerry®, Windows and most Java phones.

Application Builder – form and application builder with workflow and multi-relational database capabilities.

HyperOffice empowers organizations to quickly setup collaborative environments and communication systems in the Cloud accessible to any team member from a PC, Mac, or mobile device and without any IT resources.

There are even open-source CRM systems (like Sugar CRM) that you can host yourself on top of an IaaS Cloud. I don't consider doing so to be a SaaS Cloud, because now you are responsible for patching and backing up and upgrading and all of that business, but you could do it, if you wanted.

In this chapter, I will introduce you to some of the most popular, newest, and coolest Software as a Service solutions.

Google

We all know the search engine, Google®. They may dominate in the search engine realm, but they are also one of the biggest SaaS providers with a little consumer e-mail service called Gmail! Google really shook up the e-mail world in 2004 with the release of Gmail, its free e-mail service. Microsoft's Hotmail and Yahoo at the time were the ones that owned the marketplace, but their downfall was the 10 MB storage limit that they imposed on users. Then Google came along and announced a gigabyte of free storage with Gmail.

This is an example of a Software-as-a-Service Cloud that is experiencing tremendous growth thanks to the same benefits Google itself is realizing — scale and the ever-decreasing costs of storage hardware. Because of these benefits, a SaaS approach to delivering enterprise software is ready to tackle the traditionally-deployed models on a pure cost-savings basis alone.

But what is the advantage of Gmail? Many users say it is more full–featured than something like Microsoft Outlook® or one of the other traditional email clients. When I ask them why they say that, I get answers like:

- More storage space
- Access from anywhere
- Integrated chat

But what about security? Because most email clients reside on a laptop, the facts and figures about the number of laptops stolen in the US alone every year are staggering, especially when you consider that most of those laptops are unencrypted so access to the email client (and certainly the underlying mailbox) is readily available to thieves.

According to Google executives, 60% of corporate data resides on unprotected PCs or laptops. Here are some other facts, from datatheftsolutions.com, for you to consider as you contemplate a Cloud email service:

- 12,000 laptops are lost in U.S. airports each week, and two-thirds are never returned. Dell & Ponemon Institute, *Airport Insecurity: the case of lost laptops*, June 30, 2008
- One out of every 10 notebook computers will be stolen within the first 12 months of purchase, and 90% of them will never be recovered. – FBI
- Laptop theft related; 60% of corporate data resides on desktops and laptops – IDC
- Laptop theft accounted for 50% of reported security attacks.
- CSI, The 12th Annual Computer Crime and Security Survey, 2007

And though you may think you are safe because you are a public sector agency, most of the theft of important data comes from inside of the firewall, not the outside:

- 62% of breaches were attributed to significant internal errors. Verizon, *2008 Data Breach Investigations Report*, 2008
- The majority of data breaches (61%) originate from internal sources, as a result of enterprises' inability to enforce their IT policies or due to problems with the policies themselves. Data Monitor, *Mitigating the Risks of Data Loss*, August 2007

To bolster security Google now supports two–factor authentication, which I personally use and highly recommend. Now of course, Google is not just for email. They have an entire office suite of products available as a SaaS offering.

It appears that for cost and security reasons many agencies, especially at the state and local level, have already said "enough!" The state of Wyoming, for example, said "enough" to managing their own email servers. As a matter of fact, they went one step further. They switched not only to Gmail for email but Google Docs® for their business productivity. For a list price of $50.00 per–user per–year they were able to cease running their own applications, patching and upgrading those applications. They no longer had to procure the underlying hardware, pay maintenance for that hardware, use their own power, cooling and space for that hardware as well as provide physical security for that hardware.

Sonian

Sonian is a relatively new up-and-comer in the industry. But what they provide is a very often–needed service – email archiving and e-discovery services. Two key factors are teaming up to drive customers to Sonian:

- The volume of email is skyrocketing, growing by 500% over the last 10 years, creating storage challenges for most organizations as well as operational challenges for data security and system performance.

- There has been a dramatic increase in legal and regulatory requirements, especially as they apply to email (yes – even for public sector organizations).

Combine these two driving forces and you understand why leading industry analysts believe every organization should archive its email. But what does Sonian do that is so special? Here are some of the salient features that I think make it right for a lot of public sector organizations:

- Security. Sonian understands that security is paramount to the success of their company. That is why data is encrypted in transit and at rest with customer-specific encryption keys using 256 bit AES encryption for data stored and 99.99% guaranteed SLA. In addition, Sonian runs on top of the Amazon IaaS Cloud so they rely on Amazon's worldwide data centers offering 11 "9s" of resiliency to make sure that your data is available at all times from any location with a 99.99% SLA.

- Platform Agnostic. Sonian's platform is client-agnostic, meaning that it will archive from MS Exchange, Lotus Notes, iNotes, GroupWise, Gmail, Zimbra, Kerio, Rackspace and many other email clients.

- Ease of Use. Sonian enforces customizable retention policies to make sure that no data is lost and to prevent users from deleting any sent or received information. In addition, users can use their advanced search capability to retrieve any communications using filters, wildcards, advanced boolean, fuzzy logic and/or proximity logic operators. They also allow users to perform co-mingled searches across any content (email, attachments, and files) to ensure maximum performance and data visibility to the end user.

Like many SaaS vendors, Sonian helps you get started. They have an import/export wizard to import legacy data into the Sonian Email Archiving service. And just as important as moving to a SaaS provider is how you leave that provider should you not be happy. Sonian has that covered too, with an export wizard to allow you to export archived data to .pst, .nsf, .eml, .html, .pdf or other formats.

While we're using Sonian as an example of a SaaS platform, I thought it would be interesting to show you how robust their user interface actually is.

Figure 6-2 shows a screenshot of the default dashboard view that a user would see, which provides various statistics as well as recent history information. But the system is highly customizable. Performing a search is very simple, as seen in figure 6-3, and the search screen has all of the normal email search features that one would expect.

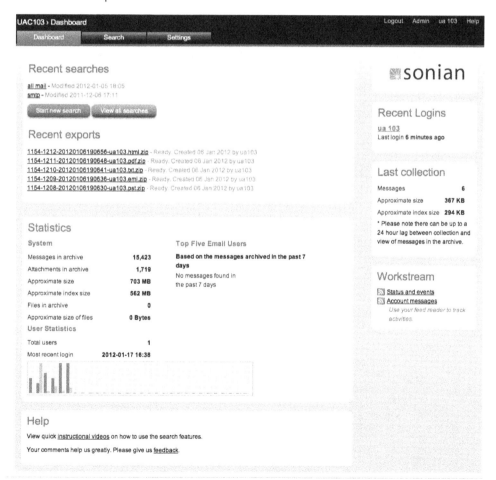

Figure 6-2: The Sonian Dashboard (© 2012 Sonian, Inc. All rights reserved).

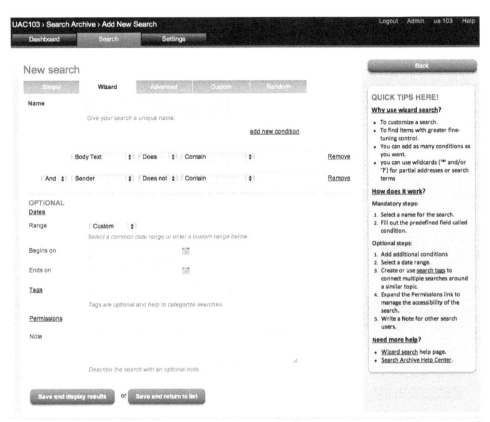

Figure 6-3: The search screen (© 2012 Sonian, Inc. All rights reserved).

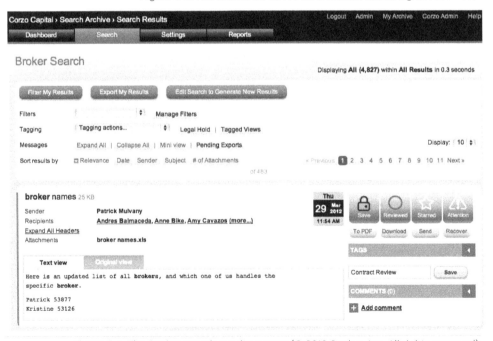

Figure 6-4: The Sonian search results screen (© 2012 Sonian, Inc. All rights reserved).

The results are just as comprehensive as those in higher-priced non-SaaS tools (figure 6-4).

There are many more features to this robust product offering and I am impressed by the product as well as the fact that it is a SaaS model. In the "My archive" screen (figure 6-5), the user sees all of their automatically-archived items in one easy interface. And because it is a SaaS model, IT doesn't have to manage all infrastructure, backups, archiving, etc.

The user can easily and quickly search their archive on any number of different fields (figure 6-6).

Figure 6-5: The My Archive Screen (© 2012 Sonian, Inc. All rights reserved).

Microsoft

Microsoft® has also gotten into the SaaS game. Microsoft Office 365 takes the industry's most recognized set of productivity (Microsoft Office®) and collaboration tools (Microsoft SharePoint®) and delivers them as a subscription service. While these tools

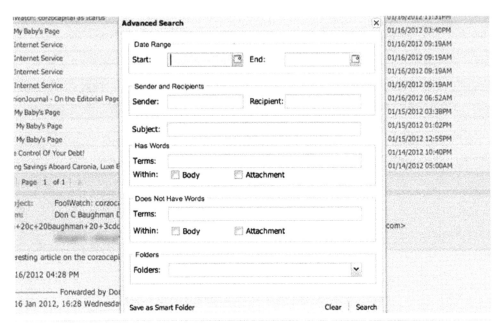

Figure 6-6: The Archive Search Screen (© 2012 Sonian, Inc. All rights reserved).

work great (we used them as part of the TechAmerica foundation for collaboration on our final Cloud2 report). In contrast to many SaaS providers, Office 365 is one of the only solutions that includes a financially-backed service level agreement, allowing you to feel confident that you chose the best Cloud solution. Microsoft Office 365 is licensed on a flexible, per-user per-month subscription plan. As with any SaaS service, your only interface is with the software itself. Microsoft manages the IT software and you control the user access rights through a portal provided by Microsoft, making it easy to scale up and scale down as needed.

There are several pieces to the Microsoft offering including:
- **Microsoft Exchange® Online** which offers email, calendar and contacts just as you probably have now with Outlook. Microsoft runs Exchange on their globally-redundant servers, protected by built-in antivirus and anti-spam filters and unlimited, IT-level phone support 24 hours a day, seven days a week. This service allows users to send and receive mail from almost anywhere and includes mobile clients for most of today's most popular smart devices as well as access from

just about any browser.

- **Microsoft SharePoint® Online** which provides a central place to share documents and information. Since it is designed to work with familiar Office applications, it's easy to save documents directly to SharePoint Online, and work together on proposals and projects because users have access to the documents and information they need from virtually anywhere. SharePoint is the defacto collaboration tool in use today. This is an online version that you access from just about any web browser.

- **Microsoft Lync® Online** is a Cloud communications service that provides presence, instant messaging, audio/video calling, and rich online meetings with audio, video, and web conferencing. Again, it connects users together from just about anywhere, using most popular mobile smart devices.

- **Microsoft Office® Web Apps** are online companions to Microsoft Word, Microsoft Excel, Microsoft PowerPoint, and Microsoft OneNote that provide users an easy way to access, view, and edit documents directly from a web browser.

So now users can stay with the apps they probably already use, and your IT staff doesn't have to worry about the underlying infrastructure, management or monitoring. As with most SaaS offerings, Microsoft has several pricing plans available depending on your size (number of users) and specific requirements.

Another Microsoft SaaS Product – Dynamics CRM Online – is a SaaS CRM platform that is not to be confused with Microsoft Dynamics CRM (without the "online" in the title) which is functionally the same software but hosted within your data center.

The Online product is available in 41 languages and 40 markets worldwide. Microsoft is making service performance and reliability a real priority with the Dynamics CRM Online product. In fact a 99.9% financially-backed service level agreement is included with every subscription.

The Microsoft Dynamics CRM Online difference:

Customer information is provided through the familiar Microsoft Outlook interface which makes it nice for users already using the Outlook client or at least familiar with it. The solution boasts the following capabilities:

- Marketing—flexible segmentation tools, simplified campaign management capabilities, intuitive response tracking, and insightful analytics.
- Sales—full lead to cash visibility, lead and opportunity tracking, streamlined approvals, and real-time sales forecasts.
- Customer Service—tools that simplify case management, streamline escalations, improve knowledge sharing, and enable more effective account management.
- Extended CRM—a flexible framework that helps organizations create custom business applications and industry solutions.[13]

HyperOffice

Finally, I wanted to take a quick look at a collaboration alternative called HyperOffice. They have already converted several state and local agencies with their plain, no-nonsense pricing, and easy-to-use service. By the time you read this, I'll bet they will have made their way into the federal arena too!

The components that make up their offering (figure 6-7) are simple and straightforward:

- Business Email—A reliable hosted business email solution with mobile and Outlook sync. Simple. Now you can get email from the SaaS Cloud provider and use your Outlook client just as you are (probably) used to now. This service comes with an online calendar and task manager.
- Online Contact Management—Whether it's from a mobile device or a plain browser, keep your contacts sync'd and up to date.

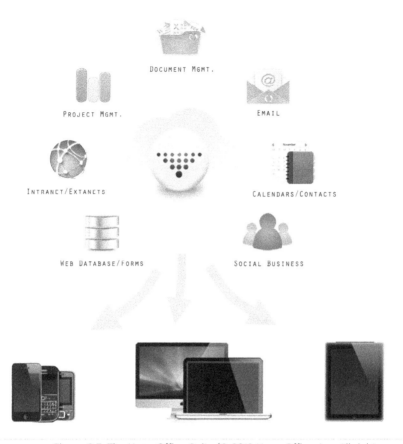

Figure 6-7: The HyperOffice Suite (© 2012 HyperOffice, Inc. All rights reserved).

- Online Document Management—A streamlined document management portal which includes file storage, document sharing and collaboration capabilities.
- Online Project Management—Manage multiple projects and globally-dispersed teams, through a centralized online project management console using just about any browser. You can even manage complex projects with multiple tasks which have elaborate inter-relationships through this same portal.

They have several pricing models to fit your needs from Core Collaboration, which only includes the basic features, to

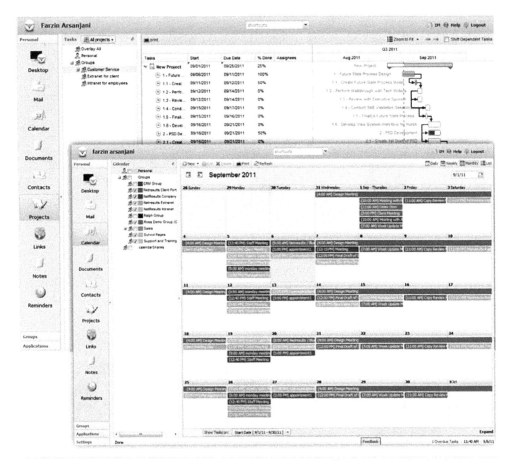

Figure 6-8: The HyperOffice Project and Calendar Screens
(© 2012 HyperOffice, Inc. All rights reserved).

Enterprise Collaboration, which gives you everything. They even have à la carte pricing for other options should you require it. Their plans scale based on number of users that are subscribed to the service each month. They have several white papers with TCO comparison data on their website (www.hyperoffice.com); in one document they claim that for 250 users they are less than one fourth of the cost of a comparable Microsoft Exchange® deployment.[14]

Once again, as with any good SaaS provider, HyperOffice has all of the services necessary to get you converted over, including email and document conversion services.

14 From the Microsoft brochure CRM Online Datasheet which can be found at
http://az26122.vo.msecnd.net/docs/CRM_Online_Datasheet.pdf

Figure 6-9: The HyperOffice Contact Screen (© 2012 HyperOffice, Inc. All rights reserved).

The user interface for HyperOffice, Figure 6-8, shows the elegant yet sophisticated Project Screen as well as the Calendar screen.

In figure 6-9, we see the screen for contacts which they call "Connect." All the details are neatly organized and presented to the user.

When we normally talk about SaaS, we talk about SaaS offerings that are hosted in a public Cloud, sometimes on top of public IaaS Clouds. HyperOffice really understands business. They understand that sometimes the information contained in an office system is proprietary information that you do not want in the public Cloud. So HyperOffice is sold both as a public SaaS offering, or a private offering to be installed behind your firewall, on a private IaaS Cloud. It is one of the many reasons why I like the product. But don't just take my word for it. Here are some of the many reviews for their product (figure 6-10).

"Overall, I was deeply impressed by HyperOffice's depth of features, tight integration of all its elements, sleek appearance, and crack support team."

"The best thing about HyperOffice is that it combines all collaboration tools into one solution, helping to avoid the web app patchwork quilt problem and keeping remote teams organized and working effectively." **The New York Times**

"CRN Test Center Review: HyperOffice a Great Solution for Cloud-based Collaboration." **CRN** TEST CENTER RECOMMENDED

InformationWeek

"InformationWeek ranks HyperOffice 9th in its Top 15 Cloud Collaboration applications."

Figure 6-10: Reviews of the HyperOffice product (from the Hyperoffice.com website)

SaaS Case Study 1 –
State of Minnesota

The agency:
Executive Branch, State of Minnesota

Their challenge:
Converting 30 email and collaboration systems to one efficient state-wide system

Their solution:
Migrating to a state-wide Microsoft Office 365 email and collaboration system

In 2010, the Executive Branch of the state of Minnesota completed an 18-month project to standardize on the Microsoft Exchange
Server 2007, converting from 30 disparate messaging environments. Because the Executive Branch for the state is made up
of more than 70 agencies and 35,000 people, this effort was a
massive undertaking involving the consolidation and migration of
both email systems and their underlying Active Directory structure. In the time it had taken them to consolidate and bring everyone up to Microsoft Exchange 2007, Microsoft Exchange 2010
had been released. They were behind the curve once again. This
forced the Office of Enterprise Technology (OET), which provides
services to improve government through the effective use of
information technology, to take another look at the best way to
deliver services to their customers. Because most of the 70 state
agencies already had their own IT departments, the migration
had been a major undertaking. There was little or no standardiza-
tion of services across the various agencies, even though many
of them interacted with one another frequently to conduct state
business. They also needed to interact with state residents, other
states, and federal agencies.

Because of the complexity of the underlying state-wide IT infrastructure, the state of Minnesota formed the Minnesota Office of
Enterprise Technology (OET) in 2005. This cabinet-level agency
was tasked with providing oversight and leadership for information and telecommunications technology policy in state government. Minnesota was one of the very first states to consolidate
all IT under one organization. In some states, this organization is
designed just for policy or oversight, but not in Minnesota. Their
goal was consolidation of functions at the state level. OET's first
priority was consolidating basic functionality of communications
and networks into an enterprise solution. Next, OET focused on
what it would take to upgrade the messaging and collaboration
functionality. Many departments were already using various
versions of SharePoint for intranet, document management, and
other collaboration solutions. Knowing that they needed a major

upgrade immediately and knowing that they did not have the funds or the resources for yet another undertaking of this size, OET began to explore the options available to them.

First, they looked at their existing email and collaboration requirements, plus the requirement to add new functionality such as presence, so state agencies and departments could collaborate more effectively.

The most obvious option available was to keep the current arrangement. But they knew that, long term, that strategy was not in the best interest of the state. They had just undertaken a major – and successful – consolidation effort, but eventually they would have to upgrade again. Their current method of doing things met most – but not all – of their requirements, and some not very well. After evaluating several other options, they determined that using a SaaS Cloud was one way of delivering a service that would meet their business requirements and promised SLAs, in a cost-effective manner.

After looking at several vendors, they determined that Microsoft's Office 365 was the best fit, creating only minor disruption to the user base since they were already Exchange users. "Really the deciding factor was not price, although we are saving about a third compared to others in similar circumstances," said Ed Valencia, Deputy Commissioner (OET) and Chief Technology Officer for the state of Minnesota. "It was all about delivering a shared service model and giving better service to our customers."

In September, 2010, the Minnesota OET had signed an agreement with Microsoft to deliver the state's enterprise-unified communications and collaboration services in a Microsoft-hosted environment. Minnesota was the first state to announce an initiative to move all employees to a Cloud-based environment.[15] They

---

15 Microsoft Case study: http://www.microsoft.com/casestudies/Microsoft-Office-365/State-of-Minnesota/State-Government-Moves-to-Hosted-Solution-to-Improve-Cross-Agency-Collaboration/4000011770

procured everything at once:
- Email
- SharePoint for collaboration
- Document management and sharing
- Presence, video and voice

There were two major challenges that preceded that announcement: security and legal. First, everything had to be approved by
the state's Security Officer. Ed said, "It took 3 or 4 months of due
diligence both on our part and working with Microsoft, but our
security folks were finally satisfied. In addition, we worked with
Microsoft to accommodate certain changes that they needed to
make for us. For example, we require that all employees who have
access to state data must be fingerprinted for security purposes.
That was not something that Microsoft had done, but they were
willing to make this change to accommodate us. There was a long
line of concessions like that and Microsoft came through for us.
That impressed us." OET believes the highly-secure architecture
of Office 365 and the state-of-the-art physical security of the data
center facilities at Microsoft dramatically increased data security.

The legal challenges centered around the procurement of SaaS
services. The state had no framework for purchasing a service
where the charges changed monthly. They had to modify their purchasing processes and procedures to accommodate that change.

Following a year-long process of testing and evaluating the solution, OET began to migrate to Office 365 in October 2011. In six
weeks, OET moved 100% of the mailboxes from Exchange Server
to Exchange Online. The successful transition included 39,000
mailboxes, 4 terabytes of data, and 66.5 million items. When the
state's employees went home one evening, they were on Outlook;
when they returned to work the next day, they were on Exchange
Online. Most did not even realize they had been migrated.
Not that there weren't issues with the migration. The long period

of testing and evaluation had revealed several issues, mostly with the state's then-current systems, policies and procedures. Throughout the testing phase these were all identified and flushed out. "The actual migration was a piece of cake once we got through all of those issues," Ed said. "Really, we just had to make our two worlds fit together." Tarek Tomes, the OET Assistant Commissioner for service strategy and delivery, told me that from a technical standpoint, the actual conversion was "an incredibly seamless journey for us. All of the upfront testing was really due in large part to the fact that as a public sector entity, our directory infrastructure is large, complex and different from those in the private sector. We had to find a way to meld the two systems together." The State also had to make some changes. They had to eliminate the unnecessary complexity that had crept into their systems over time. They reviewed things like retention policies, legal policies, executive mandates, etc. According to Tarek, "We challenged the question 'We need it like this' with 'Why?'"

With Exchange Online, the most noticeable difference for employees was additional email storage. Each employee's mailbox increased from 100 megabytes (MB) to 5 gigabytes (GB). OET also provided a larger 25 GB mailbox to a handful of employees who had unusually large storage requirements. Plus, with all employee mailboxes on Exchange Online, distribution lists could easily be created and maintained. The Governor and other executives could now send messages to all state employees in one easy step. Valencia commented, "If an emergency or another situation happens that requires an organization wide communication, for the first time our leadership can send an email to all employees in the executive branch, without IT staff having to spend significant time piecing together multiple lists. The State government shutdown in summer 2011 is a recent example where we needed to update all employees on information that was changing rapidly."[16]

---

16 ibid

With Microsoft Office 365, OET has eliminated the need for its staff to perform major – and time consuming – upgrades and build out future server and storage farms. Microsoft now takes care of the servers and software administration, including all of the common tasks associated with managing an infrastructure:
- Software and hardware installation
- Patching of systems and applications
- Implementing security updates
- Performing server/storage/ network upgrades

Using these time savings, OET now redirects the IT staff to projects that are more strategic for the state, such as helping agencies define new use cases for cross-agency collaboration. Commissioner and CIO Carolyn Parnell said, "The most remarkable thing was that Microsoft was able to provide collaboration and to provide it with near invisible migration. Now we don't worry about having to provide a utility function for our users, and my staff and I can concentrate on other higher level services." At the same time, Valencia told me, "I used to be the guy who was awakened in the middle of the night once every 3 weeks with some old system having glitches of some sort. But now, for over a year, I haven't had to worry about the email system."

The email migration is now complete with 100% uptime. The state had also transitioned 50% of its sites to SharePoint Online; it expects to complete its migration this year (2012). For OET, providing a reliable environment is critical. With the Office 365 product, Minnesota receives premium anti-spam and antivirus protection for all of their email and documents, geographically redundant Microsoft data centers, 24/7 phone support, and a financially backed, 99.9% uptime service level agreement.

Catapult Systems is seeing a lot of adoption of Office 365, not only in the state and local space, but also in the federal, civilian and DOD, spaces as well. Apollo Gonzalez, director of Emerging

Technologies told me, "At Catapult Systems we have seen a surge in demand around Microsoft's Office 365 Cloud offering. Once completed with the Office 365 Jumpstart (an offering that includes an assessment and roadmap) the majority of our customers have made the switch in order to offer better team collaboration, consistent cost structure, reduced refresh cost, and extend critical IT services such as Exchange email and unified communications via Lync to enable a growing mobile workforce."

With the shift to Office 365, the state of Minnesota Executive Branch has also opened new possibilities for cross-agency communications and collaboration to improve how it delivers citizen services. While the state itself can manage the Office 365 services locally, they rely on Microsoft to administer the hardware and software remotely in its world-class data center facilities. This combination immediately enables the IT staff to provide a flexible, highly-secure and reliable enterprise platform, while decreasing administration and costs.

Tarek believes that because private sector companies operate differently, the State OET department looked to them for performance data. "Many of them have been using Microsoft Office 365 for some time. We learned from them and compared how we operated to some of them. It was a learning curve for us, but Microsoft was there to help us along the way. Their white-glove migration service meant that we were highly successful. People came to work on Monday and they were using Microsoft Office 365. Some of the workers didn't even know. They actually came up to ask me if we had made the cutover!"

Tarek also addressed security issues that he encountered during the transition. "We did some things that I think we will find over time we didn't need to do. For example, we have dual diverse paths into the data centers. These are there for perceived security reasons, but we really don't need them and they really don't improve our security posture."

For the state of Minnesota there was a learning experience as they structured their requirements around a shared services environment. When everything is written with the view of the traditional IT data center, some of it simply doesn't fit into a shared services model. "One of the things we continue to press on is regulatory compliance," said Tarek. "As new rules and regulations are developed, we need to consider these new service models. We are continuing to look at ourselves differently - as a consumption environment versus an operating environment. In a consumption environment, there is a new collaborative ecosystem for the public sector that we have not seen before."

The biggest thing for the state seems to be the changing culture. They now have more of a private sector view – and less of a public one – of service delivery.

What is next for Minnesota? Based upon the success of this project, and because discount levels and pricing tiers were negotiated at procurement with Microsoft, OET is brokering these services to city, county and municipal governments that do not have the time or budget resources to undertake a project of this magnitude. They are already in talks with several cities and municipalities within the state. Not satisfied with one consumption model, they are continuing to evaluate other services where moving to the Cloud could meet their objectives, while continuing to put data at the users' fingertips, making them centers of innovation, rather than consumers of an infrastructure world.

According to Carolyn Parnell, the Commissioner (OET) and Chief Information Officer, state of Minnesota, "This is a shared services model at its best. Because of budget cuts, the thinking of state IT departments is changing out of necessity. We are happy to be ahead of the curve with this functionality. This is real collaboration."

Email and collaboration are two of the applications most often being moved to the Cloud right now. Cloud has become just one of many ways to deliver a service to the business or organization. It should be evaluated along with all of the other options to see which one best meets the needs of the business unit. But the evaluation should be done at the service level, not the organization level. As Ed Valencia pointed out, "Why should we put time and effort into running our own mail and collaboration system? We let the experts do that."

8

SaaS Clouds for Other Uses

SaaS Clouds can be used for email and collaboration. But they can also be used for many other types of workloads. In this chapter I'll briefly review two SaaS offerings that fall outside the email or collaboration space.

Salesforce®

Perhaps the most famous example of the SaaS Clouds is Salesforce®, which is offered by salesforce.com, inc. In 1999, Marc Benioff, the chairman and CEO of salesforce.com, inc. ("salesforce.com") founded the company with a vision to democratize enterprise technology. His mission was to revolutionize enterprise software. Benioff is regarded as the leader of what he has termed "The End of Software™," the now-proven belief that multi-tenant, Cloud computing technology delivers immediate benefits at reduced risks and costs. As a matter of fact, he was a 13-year veteran at Oracle when he realized that the future was not monolithic in-house development, but rather a simple pay-as-you-go model. Not to say that Salesforce doesn't include plenty of provisions for customization for your particular business or agency, but let's face it – how much differentiation is there between CRM systems today? They all keep track of your customers, the quotes that you have sent them, the orders they have placed, and the order status. They all let you run a bunch of reports to see how you are doing! There are nuances, but today, CRM is pretty much CRM. And that is driving the rapid adoption of SaaS, especially in enterprise applications like CRM. In fact, it is one of the many things responsible for salesforce.com's explosive growth over the past 13 years. Under Benioff's direction, salesforce.com has grown from a groundbreaking idea into a publicly-traded company that is the market and technology leader in enterprise Cloud computing. For its revolutionary approach, salesforce.com has received several awards, including:

- Forbes Most Innovative Companies
- The Wired 40
- Top Ten Disrupter by Forbes

In addition, the product itself has won numerous awards, including:

- CRM Magazine 2012 Service Leader Awards
- Software & Information Industry Association "Codie Award" for Best CRM for the past six years
- "Codie Award" for Best On-Demand Platform in 2007
- Multiple "Editor's Choice" designations from PC Magazine

And Benioff himself, who is looked upon as a luminary within this industry, has won several awards including:

- 2007 Ernst & Young Entrepreneur of the Year

- SDForum Visionary Award
- Alumni Entrepreneur of the Year by the University of Southern California (USC) Marshall School of Business
- Top 100 Most Influential People in IT survey by Eweek (Number 7)
- Top 10 Greatest IT Chief Executives by VNU

At GTSI, we use Salesforce to keep track of our customers in the public sector, plus quotes, orders, order status, and other pieces of pertinent data. While Salesforce may have started as a CRM tool, today it is the world's most popular CRM. Salesforce.com technologies include:

- Sales Cloud® which is the part of Salesforce you are probably most familiar with
- Data.com® which is a link to millions of leads from corporate data and contact information for them
- Service Cloud® which is CRM designed to be used by those that provide services
- Chatter® which allows for private, employee social networks
- Radian6™ which ties leads from social media into Salesforce Sales Cloud and Service Cloud modules
- Social Platform for the Cloud. This includes three PaaS services known as:
  - Force® – develop apps targeted at your employees
  - Heroku℠ – develop apps targeted at your customers
  - Database.com™ – a Cloud-enabled, multi-tenant database on which to develop applications

Whether looking at Salesforce for sales or services, the developers have added lots of new features to meet the varying needs of their clients, including:

- Accounts and contacts—Everything you need to know about your customers and prospects

- Chatter—A chat client to keep in touch with others in your organization
- Mobile—An mobile interface into the application
- Marketing and leads—a new feature to align sales and marketing to drive better quality leads—including leads from the social web
- Opportunities and quotes—Easily expand your pipeline and sell as a team to close deals faster.
- Approvals and workflow—Nothing should stop your sales momentum. Easily drag and drop to create and automate your processes.
- Content library—Stores all of your presentations will be in one place
- Email and calendaring—Sync with Microsoft Outlook or Gmail seamlessly
- Analytics and forecasting—View and share business insights in real time
- Partners—Connect with your direct and indirect sales channels
- AppExchange®—Connect with thousands of social enterprise apps and expert services in the world's leading Cloud computing application marketplace

They even have different pricing models, ranging from simple contact management for a department of 5 users, to an enterprise edition, to an unlimited edition which gets you access to basically everything.

Salesforce is a Cloud-based application so I can log in from anywhere on basically any device as long as I have some kind of internet connection. It's easy to sign up for a free 30-day trial. Here are a few screen shots of this CRM.

In figure 8-1 I have created an account and am about to start entering leads from my call campaign. As you can see across the top, I can chat with other users of Salesforce (even external

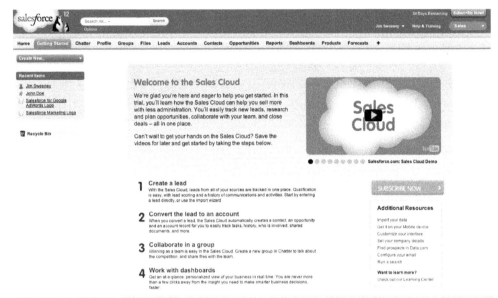

Figure 8-1: Salesforce Welcome Screen

users, if I want that feature), modify my profile, create groups of users, go through a list of my accounts or contacts, enter or view new or existing opportunities, create reports and even create forecasts based on my Salesforce CRM data, in addition to many other functions.

Figure 8-2: Salesforce.com Lead Insert screen

In figure 8-2 I am creating my first lead.

In figure 8-3, I have created my lead. As you can see at the bottom of the figure, I can record activities associated with this lead. I can keep track of all contact with this lead, track the quotes, and orders associated with this lead and (in the middle of the screen shot), use Google to map the location of this lead's address, or even send them mail with my Gmail account.

Now that my lead input is complete, you can see that the user is ready for a chat session (figure 8-4). From here, I can also invite my coworkers to chat, or the product suggests other courses of

Figure 8-3: New lead created

action in their "What to do Next" section.

In figure 8-5, we see that the product comes with an impressive array of preconfigured reports. However, you have an almost-unlimited capability to create and run your own reports to suit your specific needs. No, that does not make the Salesforce Service Cloud a Platform-as-a-Service, just a rich Cloud-based application. In other words, running a report does not equal PaaS as we

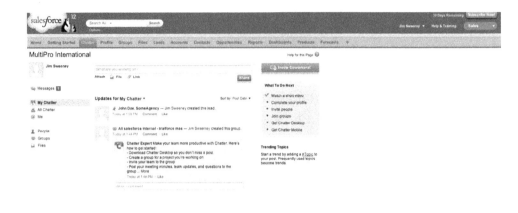

Figure 8-4: The Salesforce Chatter Screen

will see in the chapter on PaaS Clouds (Chapter 10).

Figure 8-6 shows us that salesforce.com is always introducing new features to keep it ahead of the pack. The latest addition, a forecasting section, helps users forecast throughout all phases of the sales cycle.

This product is a rich, full-featured SaaS package for users seeking a CRM tool for their organization. And remember the benefits

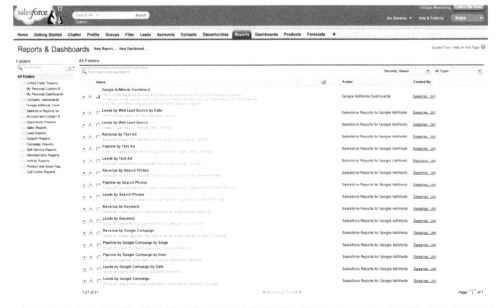

Figure 8-5: The Salesforce Reports screen

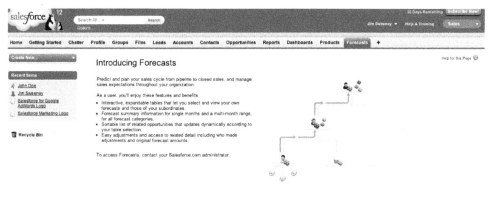

Figure 8-6: The Salesforce Forecasts screen

of a SaaS Cloud. The only interface that your users have to the SaaS Cloud is through the web-interface. All the burdens of the underlying layers (servers, storage, networking, and physical infrastructure), all of the costs associated with them (maintenance, power, cooling, and space) and all of the normal day-to-day work that is associated with these devices (configuring, patching, upgrading, and backing up) is no longer your responsibility. That is handled by salesforce.com. Oh, and did I mention that they already have a mobile tool for all you mobile users out there?

Ok. But what about security? How can you be sure that salesforce.com will implement the security policies necessary to ensure that your data is safe and secure? Salesforce.com handles physical security, with features (from the company's website at trust.salesforce.com) like:

- Access control and physical security
- 24-hour manned security, including foot patrols and perimeter inspections
- Biometric scanning for access
- Dedicated concrete-walled data center rooms
- Computing equipment in access-controlled steel cages
- Video surveillance throughout facility and perimeter
- Building engineered for local seismic, storm, and flood risks
- Tracking of asset removal
- Fire detection and suppression

- VESDA (very early smoke detection apparatus)
- Dual-alarmed, dual-interlock, multi-zone, pre-action dry pipe water-based fire suppression

Then they take care of the environmental controls with not only humidity and temperature control but a redundant (N+1) cooling system.

After that they look at the power requirements for their data centers with features like:
- Underground utility power feed
- Redundant (N+1) CPS/UPS systems
- Redundant power distribution units (PDUs)
- Redundant (N+1) diesel generators with on-site diesel fuel storage

For network connectivity they look at security around the network layer with:
- Concrete vaults for fiber entry
- Redundant internal networks
- Network neutral; connects to all major carriers and located near major Internet hubs
- High bandwidth capacity

That takes care of the lowest level of security, but what about all users that are connecting from elsewhere? Salesforce.com secures that transmission of data ensuring that connection to their environment is via SSL 3.0/TLS 1.0, using global step-up certificates from Verisign, ensuring that users have a secure connection from their browsers to the Salesforce.com service. In addition, individual user sessions are identified and re-verified with each transaction, using a unique token created during the login process.

Of course, they provide the standard network protection, including:

- Perimeter firewalls and edge routers block unused protocols
- Internal firewalls segregate traffic between the application and database tiers
- Intrusion detection sensors throughout the internal network report events to a security event management system for logging, alerts, and reports
- A third-party service provider continuously scans the network externally and alerts changes in baseline configuration

How does salesforce.com handle disaster recovery? They take the following steps to ensure they will still be up in the event of a disaster:

- The Salesforce service performs real-time replication to disk at each data center, and near real-time data replication between the production data center and the disaster recovery center
- Data are transmitted across encrypted links
- Disaster recovery tests verify projected recovery times and the integrity of the customer data

Finally, for backups, salesforce.com lists the following security features:

- All data are backed up to tape at each data center, on a rotating schedule of incremental and full backups
- The backups are cloned over secure links to a secure tape archive
- Tapes are not transported offsite and are securely destroyed when retired

The security steps that salesforce.com is taking are adequate for all but the most sensitive/classified data. As part of the evaluation criteria of a SaaS provider, I recommend that you look not only at the features that are available as part of the product to ensure that the product meets your needs, but also evaluate the security features of the company to ensure that you are satisfied with the integrity and safety of your data. And, it should also be noted, if that SaaS provider runs on top of someone else's IaaS Cloud, as many do, then the evaluation should continue down to the IaaS provider as well.

GCE

Global Computer Enterprises (GCE) provides an accounting and financial management platform for the public sector. It's offered as a Software-as-a-Service delivery model. GCE's Cloud gives customers the ability to achieve high levels of functionality on day one without the cost and risks associated with building a system from scratch. Once again, you need not worry about the underlying hardware on which the platform operates, you don't have to keep the software up-to-date or patched, and you need not worry about the backup of your data. So you get the functionality that your organization needs today, and into the future, with significant cost savings. In fact, this company has been so successful that they now offer three core products:

- The GCE Financial Management Cloud
- The GCE Acquisition Management Cloud
- The GCE Asset Management Cloud

Each of these products offers a robust toolset for managing procurement, assets, and accounting and financial functions for small and large organizations. Finally, GCE now offers a mobile service for smart devices that provides access to the customer's data, with functionality to look-up, search and approve/disapprove requisitions and obligations documents. How many current financial management systems have that capability?

The GCE Financial Management System already includes:
- Oracle Federal Financials R12
- Sunflower Assets
- GCE's Finance and Procurement Desktop for simplified acquisitions credit card reconciliation, warranty management, and receipts

- CompuSearch PRISM contract writing system
- MarkView electronic imaging and invoice management
- SharePoint
- JIRA
- Microsoft Project for document management and tracking.

In addition, GCE delivers an enterprise reporting tool that includes dozens of canned reports, an easy-to-use ad hoc reporting tool, plus multiple search capabilities.

GCE provides a full range of services to help customers transition to the Cloud including project management, data migration, legacy systems integration, change management/training, as well as help desk/onsite support, audit support, and transactional processing services.

The GCE Cloud has out-of-the-box integration with FPDS-NG, CCR, FedBizOpps, ORCA, FedConnect, and USASpending.gov, and includes the following modules (figure 8-7):

Budget Execution	General Ledger Management	Accounts Payable
Accounting Period Maintenance	Payroll Management	Vendor Management
Receivables Management	Travel Management	Purchase Cards
Payment Processing	Reimbursable Services	Project Management
Reporting and Search Services	Financial Reports	Working Capital Fund
	Ad Hoc Query Tool	Data Extracts

Figure 8-7: The GCE SaaS Financial Management System - Modules

I met Mare Lucas, VP Business Development for GCE, when we both served on the TechAmerica Cloud2 commission together. At that time I was impressed that a public sector organization such as the Department of Labor had implemented their software. Are you concerned about security in the Cloud? This customer trusted a Public Cloud with all of their financial data! And let's not stop with security. Can you imagine the costs of abandoning a legacy financial management system, retraining workers, and migrating data from the old system to the new one. I was so captivated by this story that I asked Mare if I could write about her company and her customer. Read more about this transition in our upcoming case study on the Department of Labor.

Summary

That wraps up our look at the SaaS delivery model and some of the most popular SaaS providers, both for email and collaboration as well as other software out there today. Certainly there are many others. By the time you read this, there will probably be even more. Are they right for you? It depends on your requirements and the sensitivity of your data. A good understanding of what each vendor provides, how they are priced, what SLA's they are willing to sign up to, and a deep understanding of how they handle security are all important factors when making this decision.

SaaS Case Study 2 –

US Department of Labor

The agency:
United States Department of Labor

Their challenge:
To modernize an aging financial system that did not meet current accounting and financial standards

Their solution:
Adopt a SaaS model developed by a commercial vendor for financial management

Between 2003 and 2008, the Department of Labor spent $35 million to upgrade and replace an old financial system which failed to comply with current statutory and regulatory requirements.[17] For the Department of Labor, the solution was moving to a SaaS model for financial management developed by a commercial vendor. In Capitol Hill testimony, James L. Taylor, the Department's Chief Financial Officer said:

> "When this previous effort failed, the Department awarded a contract for the development and implementation of the Department's New Core Financial Management System (New Core or NCFMS) in July 2008, with a goal of replacing the legacy system which had been in use for over two decades. New Core is based upon a pre-configured software suite that is commercially available."[18]

In truth, the problem was more pervasive than at just the Department of Labor. On June, 28th, 2010, Executive Office of the President Director Peter R. Orszag issued a MEMORANDUM FOR HEADS OF EXECUTIVE DEPARTMENTS AND AGENCIES. In it, he states that:

"Federal Information Technology (IT) projects too often cost more than they should, take longer than necessary to deploy, and deliver solutions that do not meet our business needs. Although these problems exist across our IT portfolio, financial systems modernization projects in particular have consistently underperformed in terms of cost, schedule, and performance.

"To address these problems, the White House Chief of Staff and I today signed a Memorandum launching an IT project management reform effort. As part of this effort, OMB is concurrently issuing this guidance that requires all CFO Act agencies to immediately halt the issuance of new task orders or new procurements for all financial system projects, pending review and approval

---

17 http://republicans.edlabor.house.gov/UploadedFiles/12.07.10_taylor.pdf
18 ibid

from OMB. This guidance also:
- Sets forth guiding principles for the acquisition and project management of new financial systems;
- Specifies the procedures for an immediate review and evaluation of current financial system modernization projects; and
- Clarifies and updates OMB policies on financial management shared services, financial system standards, and financial software testing and certification."[19]

This memo established an OMB review process for all financial system modernization projects with $20 million or more in planned spending for development or modernization. In addition, this directive covered agencies that had previously completed modernization projects. They were instructed to refrain from moving into additional rounds of planning and development until OMB had approved a revised implementation plan for those projects. It further stated that, "OMB may review systems that have completed implementation when a failure occurs (e.g., the system fails in performing basic functions)."[20]

In regard to Shared Services, the memo had this to say: "OMB supports shared service arrangements when cost effective, but will no longer mandate them in all cases for financial management systems...OMB expects that requirements to re-scope agency modernization projects contained in this guidance will enable greater adoption of shared service arrangements with lower risk and greater cost impacts. Further, financial management shared service efforts will now focus on the higher impact area of transaction processing."[21]

In June of 2008, nearly two years before the OMB Memorandum was issued, the Department of Labor (DOL) chose a FSIO-compliant financial management service from Global Computer Enterprises (GCE) offered as a SaaS Cloud offering. GCE was able

19 June 28, 2010 Executive Office of the President. Memorandum for Heads of Executive Departments and Agencies M-10-26
20, 21 ibid

to provision the Department of Labor on its Cloud in 18 months for less than half of the $35M they previously spent. Even more impressive, the implementation included a total of 12 agencies and 12 payment centers. "The problem was not so much the age of the current system, but rather the fact that it did not support the latest accounting standards," said David Lucas, Chief Strategy Officer for GCE. "This forced the agency into manual process workarounds which made the old system very cumbersome and inefficient. We took them off an old COBOL system running on a mainframe that did not integrate with other systems. In addition, there was no granularity of data with the old system because of its age. It was really just a general ledger system and not a full financial management system."

Today, Department of Labor is running a modern system with Oracle Federal Financials version R12 at its heart, to deliver real-time integration across the agency, as well as fully-automated controls and sub-ledgers. Through the GCE service, the Department of Labor has provided their financial community with a toolset to automate and streamline their daily tasks, while adding multiple levels of waste, fraud and abuse controls. This toolset includes key features such as electronic invoicing and an enterprise-level reporting tool. The GCE service also eliminated the headache of managing and funding hardware and software, enabling the organization to focus on financial management and not IT resources.

CFO Taylor was impressed. Again from his testimony:
"The Department was able to eliminate much of its risk by contracting for a product that was already in use within the Federal government, while also reducing development costs and accelerating the timeline for implementation. The Department does not own any hardware or software associated with NewCore, eliminating the need for costly infrastructure, maintenance, and in-house technical resources dedicated to system maintenance.

New Core took 18 months to implement at an initial cost of less than $15 million, and an annual operational cost of approximately $20 million in program year 2010 and $11 million in program year 2011, and would have been in alignment with the recent OMB directive on systems modernization."

Those weren't the only benefits of the new system. Now the agency had complete granularity in all of their reports. For example, every day the system issues a report showing where money is being spent, and details what is being spent this period versus last period.

Lucas said, "Now suddenly, they have data that is coherently segregated and allows you to very easily pull information out and get something useful." The level of complexity for this project was very high because each of the 12 agencies within the Department of Labor wanted its particular issues, gaps, and legacy systems to be addressed. Eventually, more than 25 years of data was migrated into the system and more than 2,000 users across the country were trained.

DOL faced its share of challenges along the way. The first hurdle was that the anticipated number of users started at 500, fewer than 200 of whom were accounting and financial staff. That number has dramatically increased due to several factors: at the time of launch, many legacy and cuff systems were eliminated by using the new toolset, creating a much larger user population than DOL anticipated. Because of the self-service reporting tool, a much larger reports user community eventually emerged.

"The Cloud is built for that kind of scaling," said Mare Lucas, who is also Director of GCE's Change Management Practice. "The customer had to pay a modest increase to accommodate this rise in users, but certainly dramatically less of an increase than would have been dictated if they had to run out, buy and install the infrastructure to support that within such a short timeframe. After all, the architecture as well as the business model was already in place. In other words, they didn't have to stop and wait for a new license when they increased from 200 to 201 users."

David noted, "Once you have taken away the care and feeding of an enterprise system, where you must devote resources to mundane daily tasks, and move from that to SLAs and the monitoring of the SLAs (Does the help desk answer when it should? Is the system up when it should be?), you can do more with fewer people. Then you can transfer the power of people who used to run reports to analyzing reports. You can now turn data into information."

The next hurdle was agency-wide skepticism. "Because they had already failed a couple of times, there was an increased level of cynicism there," said Mare. "The Cloud gave them the certainty that they were going live. The only questions were: are people going to be ready and is the organization as a whole going to be ready? The Cloud model means that you are going to use something that is commoditized, so you have a much more likelihood of success. The standards are there because the Federal government has spent many years defining the standards. The intent is to not be special!"

Training was also a major issue. Imagine having to retrain thousands of employees who were accustomed to using the old system. To minimize the impact of change, GCE conducted hundreds of workshops across the country to familiarize end-users with the features and services of the new system. Throughout implementation, GCE continued to hold events to give users the opportunity to see and touch the new system, including webinars for field users of the large integrating systems such as procurement, grants, and travel systems. GCE even rolled out a "sandbox" where users could log into the system with migrated data and take it for a test run. They also conducted two rounds of training: the first round trained users by business process area; the second round delivered on-site, agency-specific, hands-on training for the 12 Department of Labor agencies, as well as pre-launch support at each regional finance center. By launch time, thousands of users across the country had participated in training sessions designed to minimize the impact of the changeover and ensured that users would be operational in the new system.

"This is a new model. There are areas where you have to be flexible," said David. "When we went live there were backlogs in some areas. Some of them were data migration issues where the data was not as granular as our system required, so it took more time to migrate. Change management was also a very big piece of the pie. As a service provider, you can't just sit back and say 'the software works.' You have to rally and bring a team on-site and create new ways of learning. We had to adapt in order to get the job done. Sometimes it was shoulder-to-shoulder with agency staff; sometimes it was becoming more innovative in the way we taught. Cloud doesn't take all that away."

Now in its third year of operation, the Department of Labor is receiving even greater added value from GCE. New requests keep coming in such as "Give me my data on my mobile devices," or "Help me find ways to add more automation via tools into my processes." David explained, "Whenever these requests come in, the agency doesn't have to start from scratch. In fact, it is an added feature of the SaaS model that everyone benefits from the development that we are doing for one customer. In custom-developed systems, a user of one financial management system may want an additional feature but the user of another other system does not. In this model, by default, when we develop a new feature for one customer, it is available to all customers".

This system has been so successful that in June of 2011, just 6 months after his previous appearance before Congress, CFO Taylor was able to report:
"I am pleased to report that the Department's independent auditor, retained under contract by the Department's Inspector General, has in fact issued an unqualified, or 'clean,' opinion on

the Department's FY 2010 consolidated financial statements. An unqualified opinion is the most favorable of financial audit outcomes and means that the financial statements present fairly, in all material respects, the financial position, results of operations, and cash flows of the audit identity in conformity with generally accepted accounting principles. Critically, this opinion must be issued by an independent, expert, third party who adheres to strict auditing and ethical standards.

As a result of the revised opinion we obtained late last month, the Department now has received an unqualified opinion on its financial statements for 14 consecutive fiscal years. The American people can continue to have confidence in the Department's financial operations and stewardship of the resources with which it has been entrusted. The Department's revised FY 2010 Agency Financial Report has been distributed to the Department's various Congressional oversight committees and posted to the Department's public website."[22]

He commented further:
"While I am proud that we were able to achieve an unqualified opinion, I am also aware that there is significant work left to do. Both the original and revised FY 2010 audit reports note four areas that remain in need of the Department's attention. I can report today that we have made significant progress in resolving or mitigating many of the concerns leading to these findings.

Over the past six months we have continued to work to normalize the Department's financial operations and resolve outstanding data integrity issues arising from the integration of a number of existing legacy systems into a new, modern financial management environment. We are addressing system functionality, making operations more efficient and effective for users, and continuing user outreach and training efforts. While there is still work to do in all of these areas, we are buoyed by the unqualified, clean opinion we received from the independent auditor and we will build from this experience as we continue to strengthen the Department's financial management environment."

CFO Taylor did not stop there with his praise of the system. In the Fiscal 2011 Department of Labor Annual Report, he said:

"Transparency and accountability provide the foundation for effective financial management. Because we finished our transition to a new core financial management system, Department of Labor officials have taken a major step toward the administration's goal of providing clearer and more accessible information to stakeholders. We have modernized government through technology.

The FY 2011 financial statements are the first produced entirely from the new financial system, and I am proud that the Department has obtained an unqualified audit opinion on its financial statements for 14 consecutive fiscal years. This clean audit opinion provides independent confirmation that the Department's financial statements are presented fairly and in conformity with generally-accepted accounting principles. Accurate and timely financial information improves DOL's accountability to its stakeholders and the operational, budget, and policy decision-making processes that are the foundation for the services the Department delivers to the public."

David Lucas elaborated on why this model succeeded, "The fact is, many smart people and smart companies tried to do this before, but it was really the wrong model. Building financial management systems from scratch is really risky. Other agencies have also failed and many others have struggled. Here is the same software that is already done which meets at least 80% of the requirements that any agency would require of it."

When asked about security, Mare Lucas said, "Security is not an issue in financial management systems. All of the data is sensitive but unclassified (there are some exceptions, but very few). In addition, financial data is already highly regulated (FISMA, SAS70, IT audits). So you are really at the point where service providers' investment in security will shortly outpace what the government will spend on security. That makes it attractive to move your data to a public Cloud provider."

Each year, AGA recognizes two elected or presidentially appointed Federal officials who exemplify and promote excellence in government management and have demonstrated outstanding leadership in enhancing sound financial management legislation, regulations, practices, policies and systems, and made outstanding contributions to enhancing government financial management. Recently, Department of Labor CFO James L. Taylor was honored with the distinguished Federal Leadership Award at AGA's National Leadership Conference. He was recognized for his effective leadership in promoting departmental and governmental financial management excellence and improved operations through efficiency and performance enhancements within the Departments of Labor, Commerce, Homeland Security, and the Federal Emergency Management Agency.

I congratulate Mr. Taylor on this tremendous achievement.

This is a great example of an agency that said, "we have spent enough" and moved to a SaaS offering with great success. There are many SaaS offerings out there. The question that you must ask is: "Are there software applications within our agency that can successfully be moved to a SaaS offering?" Certainly not all of them will lend themselves to SaaS, but there will undoubtedly be a few where significant savings and enhanced capabilities can be realized in the SaaS world.

10

Platform as a Service Clouds (PaaS)

In this chapter we'll discuss Platform-as-a-Service Clouds. Platform-as-a-Service Clouds allow developers to develop Cloud-ready applications without worrying about the underlying infrastructure. Many of them have become quite the eco-system allowing for all sorts of different development tools. It's not just for C and C++ development anymore. Now Ruby on Rails™, Database development, and even Distributed Computing development (with a Java-based software framework called Hadoop™) can be accomplished in the Cloud. We will take a look at some of the more popular PaaS Cloud offerings, including Google's PaaS offering, the Oracle PaaS Cloud offering and the Microsoft Windows Azure platform.

Just to remind ourselves what PaaS is and what it is not, let's look at figure 10-1. As you can see, the underlying infrastructure is already taken care of in the PaaS construct. PaaS offerings facilitate the deployment of applications without the cost and complexity of buying and managing the underlying hardware and software and provisioning hosting capabilities. They provide all of the facilities required to support the complete life cycle of building and delivering web applications and services in one complete package.

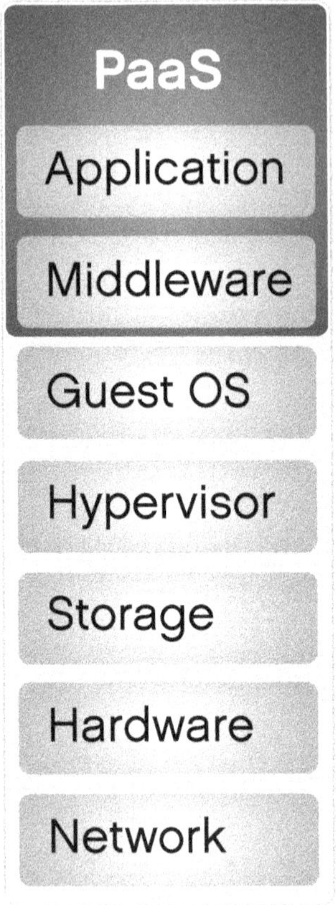

Interestingly enough this type of Cloud can be broken into a couple of different categories:

Figure 10-1: The PaaS Cloud

Add-On Development Facilities

These facilities allow customization of existing Software-as-a-Service (SaaS) applications, and in some ways are the equivalent of macro language customization facilities provided with packaged software applications such as Lotus Notes, or Microsoft. Very often, these require PaaS developers and their users to purchase subscriptions to the underlying SaaS application.

Stand-Alone Development Environments

Stand-alone PaaS environments do not include technical, licensing or financial dependencies on specific SaaS applications or web services. They are intended to provide a generalized development environment.

Once again, there are lots of offerings in this category. That adds to your choices and your flexibility, but it also adds to the confusion. Take for example, VMware. They recently announced their PaaS platform called Cloud Foundry. As a matter of fact, they went one step further announcing CloudFoundry.com as well as the open-source CloudFoundry.org. Their aim is to make a "multi-Cloud" PaaS offering enabling you to develop once but move your code seamlessly to other PaaS providers, thus preventing you the customer from experiencing vendor lock in. As I said, this also confuses the issue greatly. When we talk about VMware we normally think of a private or hybrid Cloud offering (which we will discuss in chapter 16), but here they are with a great PaaS offering with robust development environments supporting many programming languages and aiming for the higher ideal of code portability between PaaS vendors. Here we are going to look at some of the more established PaaS vendors, but for more information about the VMware offering, just go to www.CloudFoundry.com.

Oracle

Oracle® made a big announcement in the fall of 2011 with the announcement of their public Cloud offering. They have an interesting twist to their offering.
If you look at their site,[23] you will see three SaaS offerings:
- Fusion CRM – a popular customer relationship management software package
- Fusion HCM – a human capital management package
- The Oracle Social Network – a secure collaboration tool featuring text, content, video, and voice all within a single stream.

It also has some other interesting features: you can connect to your CRM and HCM applications from within it, you can connect it to your social media sites, and both internal groups as well as external groups can be tied together using it. But these are SaaS offerings and we are talking about PaaS offerings in this chapter. That is true. Right alongside the SaaS offerings are two PaaS offerings, the Java PaaS Cloud and the Database PaaS Cloud. Let's take a quick look at each one:

The Database PaaS Cloud

The Database PaaS Cloud allows you to develop Oracle applications from anywhere using DB instances in the Cloud (Oracle 11g R2). It has several unique features:

- You can develop, test and deploy using a simple monthly subscription (which we all know by now is what Cloud is about)
- You can instantly provision and deploy applications with fully managed operations and infrastructure
- You can deploy your data and application code in the Oracle Cloud or on premise in your own data center.
- You get access to all of the standards-based development tools that you are accustomed to using including Java, RESTful Web services, and Oracle APEX.

Oracle has included the Oracle Application Express (APEX) browser-based rapid application development tool so you can create and manage database objects, build database-centric applications, deploy freely provided business productivity applications and publish RESTful Web Services. The system is highly redundant and highly available and includes security features like encrypted storage (automatically and without the need to program it) and single sign-on identity management. They also provide something called Data Pump Data Loading which allows you to load data, PL/SQL and security privileges into the service and Data Object Browsing which provides Explorer-like access to all your data objects.

The Java PaaS Cloud

The Java PaaS Cloud is the other PaaS offering from Oracle. Again, it allows you to deploy in minutes, it provides you:

- WebLogic Application Server on top of which you build your Java applications
- The Oracle ADF (Application Development Framework), and

many others
- The ability to move code between the public Cloud and your private infrastructure.

Oracle has also included some other interesting features:
- WebLogic Cluster Servers to increase application reliability
- A Directory Service component so you can manage users, groups and roles with the integrated LDAP Server
- A Single Sign-On component
- The ability to run other frameworks including Spring, Hibernate and EclipseLink
- An Enterprise Manager console to monitor and manage WebLogic Servers

Right now the Oracle Fusion CRM Cloud Service and Oracle Fusion HCM Cloud Service are fully available, but Oracle Database, Java, and Social Network Cloud Services are available under "preview availability." They will be fully released in the very near future.

The applications and databases developed and deployed in the Oracle Public Cloud are portable and can be easily moved to and/or from a private Cloud or on-premise environment. It's a really interesting move that makes sense on a lot of levels for Oracle. They already have the world's bestselling database, the Java development platform and, as of last year, the Oracle Exalogic Elastic Cloud™ and Oracle Exadata™ Database Machine, so putting all of this together into a public offering just seems like the next logical evolutionary step for them.

Google App Engine

Google App Engine lets you develop and run web applications on Google's infrastructure. Applications are easy to build, easy to maintain, and easy to scale as your traffic and data storage needs grow. And, as we already know, there are no servers to maintain: you just upload your application, and it's ready to deliver to your users.

"But where do I host my web application?" You can serve your app from your own domain name using Google Apps. And you have complete flexibility to share your application with the entire world, or limit access to include only members of your organization.

Google App Engine supports applications that are written in several programming languages, including Java (using the Google Apps Java runtime environment) and Python (using one of the two Python runtime environments). Finally, App Engine provides a Go (the Google-developed concurrent programming language) runtime environment that runs natively-compiled Go code.

Like any good Cloud provider, you only pay for what you use. There are no set-up costs and no recurring fees. The resources your application uses, such as storage and bandwidth, are measured by the gigabyte, and billed at competitive rates. You maintain complete control over the maximum amounts of resources that your application can consume making budgeting easy.

Best of all, Google App Engine costs nothing to get started. All applications can use up to 1 GB of storage and enough CPU and bandwidth to support an efficient app serving around 5 million page views a month, absolutely free. When you enable billing for your application, your free limits are raised, and you only pay for resources you use above the free levels.[24]

The benefits of the Google App Engine environment are numerous:
- Dynamic (as opposed to static) web serving, with full support for common web technologies
- Persistent storage with queries, sorting and transactions

---

24 From the Google website: http://code.google.com/appengine/docs/whatisgoogleappengine.html

- Automatic scaling and load balancing
- APIs for authenticating users and sending email using Google Accounts
- A fully featured local development environment with test capability that simulates Google App Engine on your computer
- Task queues for performing work outside of the scope of a web request
- Scheduled tasks for triggering events at specified times and regular intervals
- Complete integration with your Google Accounts so that you can use the same features with members of your organization and Google Apps account

Google App Engine provides a variety of services that enable you to perform common operations when managing your application. The following APIs are provided to access these services:

- **URL Fetch**: Applications can access resources on the Internet, such as web services or other data, using App Engine's URL fetch service. The URL fetch service retrieves web resources using the same high-speed Google infrastructure that retrieves web pages for many other Google products.

- **Mail**: Applications can send email messages using App Engine's mail service. The mail service uses Google infrastructure to send email messages.

- **Memcache**: The Memcache service provides your application with a high performance in-memory key-value cache that is accessible by multiple instances of your application. Memcache is useful for data that does not need the persistence and transactional features of the datastore, such as temporary data or data copied from the datastore to the cache for high speed access.

- **Image Manipulation**: The Image service lets your application manipulate images. You have the ability to resize, crop, rotate and flip images in JPEG and PNG formats[25]

Applications run in a secure environment that provides limited access to the underlying operating system. (Remember figure 11-1). These limitations allow App Engine to distribute HTTP requests for the application across multiple servers, and start and stop servers to meet traffic demands. This sandbox approach isolates your application in its own secure environment that is independent of the hardware, operating system and physical location of the web server, which of course, is what you would expect from a Cloud-based PaaS platform. Examples of these security features include:

- An application can only access other computers on the Internet through the provided URL fetch and email services. Other computers can only connect to the application by making HTTP (or HTTPS) requests on the standard ports.

- Applications cannot write to the file system in any of the runtime environments. An application can read files all it wants, but only those files that you have uploaded with the application code. That does not mean that there is not persistent storage. There is. But your application must use the provided App Engine datastore, memcache or other service for all data that persists between requests.

- Application code can only run three ways: in response to a web request, a queued task, or a scheduled task. In addition the application code must return response data within 60 seconds, and request handlers cannot spawn a sub-process or execute code after the response has been sent.

These are some very powerful security features.

The Google App Engine does basically one thing and it does it very well. You can deploy highly scalable web applications. Compared to other scalable hosting services such as Amazon EC2, App Engine provides the infrastructure to make it easy to write scalable applications, but can only run a limited range of applications designed for that infrastructure. And that's OK.

---

25 From the Google website: http://code.google.com/appengine/docs/whatisgoogleappengine.html

Because if you need to write a web app, you can write and deploy it quickly and easily using Google App Engine without worrying about the underlying infrastructure. Google App Engine even includes an auto-scaling feature. For a good example of this feature, look at an interesting website called: **http://www.officialroyalwedding2011.org/**. This was developed by Accenture at the request of and in cooperation with the Royal Family. Why is this a good example of the need for auto-scaling? As the wedding approached, more and more people got interested in what was happening. They wanted to find out about her dress, the service, the procession route, etc. After the event people wanted to see videos and other information of the events of the day. However, you can imagine that many more people were interested in these events right before and right after the event than they were one year before the event or even a year after. The demand probably closely approximated a standard bell curve. By deploying using the Google App engine, Accenture had an autoscaling web application right out of the gate! They didn't have to anticipate demand, or provision enough services ahead of time, of even monitor and proactively manage the scaling process. The Google App Engine handled that automatically for them!

At the same time, the Google App Engine's infrastructure removes many of the system administration and development challenges of building applications to scale to hundreds of requests per second and beyond. Google handles deploying code to a cluster, monitoring, failover, and launching application instances as necessary.

Microsoft

Earlier we talked a little about the Microsoft Dynamics CRM Online offering as well as the Office 365 offering. But Microsoft also has a PaaS environment called Microsoft Windows Azure™. Windows Azure is a Cloud platform that enables you to quickly build, deploy and manage applications across the global network of Microsoft-managed data centers. You can build applications using any language, tool or framework and you can even integrate your public Cloud applications that you have developed with Azure with your existing IT environment. The Windows Azure client libraries are available for multiple programming languages, and are released under an open source license and hosted on GitHub.

Of course, like any PaaS Cloud offering, Microsoft takes care of the underlying infrastructure, but they do offer a 99.95% monthly SLA (Microsoft has separate SLA's for computer, storage, SQL, Service Bus, Access Control, Caching and Content Distribution Network).[26]

Windows Azure really consists of three parts:
- Windows Azure Compute
- Windows Azure Data Services which include:
  - SQL Azure
  - Windows Azure Storage
  - Windows Azure CDN (Content Delivery Network)
- Windows Azure Middleware Services which include:
  - AppFabric Caching
  - AppFabric Access Control Server
  - AppFabric Service Bus

Of course, on top of these three parts is your application!

The Application Philosophy of the Windows Azure Platform is based around "Design for Failure" with features such as:
- Scale out for capacity
- Scale out for redundancy
- Asynchronous communication
- Short time outs with retries

---

26 Windows Azure SLA's which can be found at: http://www.windowsazure.com/en-us/support/sla/

- Idempotent operations[27]
- Stateless with durable external storage

In the Windows Azure vernacular, an application is called a "service." This service is where you store configuration and definition information. In addition, each service will have at least one "role". A role is a collection of code with an entry point that runs in its own virtual machine. And all of the applications that you run on top of the Windows Azure Platform can be fronted with the provided Load Balancer.

Let's look at some of the storage characteristics in Windows Azure Storage. First, it's durable in that data is replicated three times. Second, it is scalable (in terms of both capacity and throughput), highly available, and uses simple and familiar programming interfaces, including both REST (HTTP and HTTPS) as well as .NET accessible. Within the storage construct you have three options:

- <u>Blobs</u> which provide a simple interface for storing named files along with metadata for the file
- <u>Tables</u> which provide lightly structured storage with a set of entities that contain a set of properties
- <u>Queues</u> which provide reliable storage and reliable delivery of messages

Just as I like the Google App Engine offering, I like the Microsoft Windows Azure Platform.

In summary, we have looked at a couple of PaaS platforms that are available today. There are many others. Determine which one is right for you by looking at the following:

1. In what language am I going to write it? (Azure supports .NET, but Google App Engine does not, for example)
2. What kind of database, if any, do you need?

---

27 Idempotent is defined as operations which performed more than once, yield the same results as if they were performed one time.

3. What security is provided? Are you comfortable with the amount of security provided given the application that you need to write and the data that will be resident in the SaaS Cloud.

4. Do you need or want to monitor and/or manage the underlying guest OS and some of the other functions (like load balancing or auto-scaling)?

Getting Started with Google App Engine

Getting started with Google App Engine is a very simple process. The first step is to log into the development environment, which I did in figure 11-1.

Then, by simply clicking on the "Create Application" button near the bottom, I was taken to figure 11-2.

Once I entered my phone number and clicked the "Send" button, I was presented the screen in figure 11-3 and in a few seconds I was texted a verification code which I then entered. Note this step only needs to be performed once.

I was then presented with the "Create

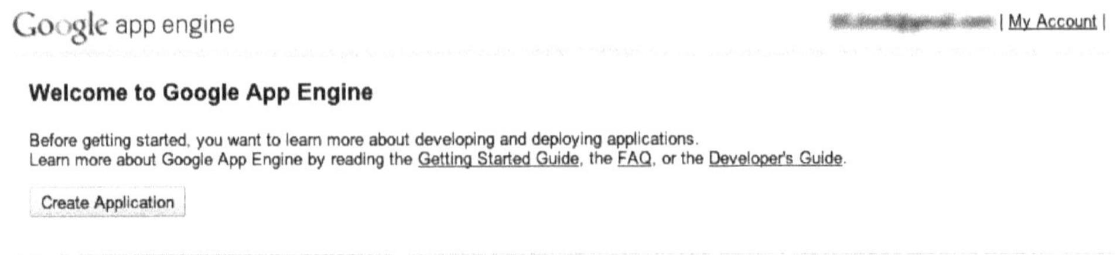

Google app engine | My Account |

Welcome to Google App Engine

Before getting started, you want to learn more about developing and deploying applications.
Learn more about Google App Engine by reading the Getting Started Guide, the FAQ, or the Developer's Guide.

Create Application

Figure 11-1: The Google App Engine Login Screen

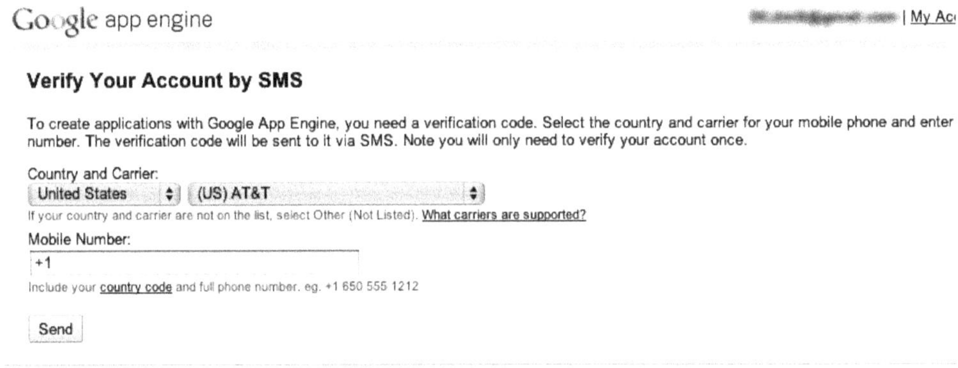

Google app engine | My Acc

Verify Your Account by SMS

To create applications with Google App Engine, you need a verification code. Select the country and carrier for your mobile phone and enter number. The verification code will be sent to it via SMS. Note you will only need to verify your account once.

Country and Carrier:
United States ⬍ (US) AT&T ⬍
If your country and carrier are not on the list, select Other (Not Listed). What carriers are supported?
Mobile Number:
+1
Include your country code and full phone number. eg. +1 650 555 1212

Send

Figure 11-2: The Google App Engine Verification Screen

Google app engine | My Acc

An Authentication Code Has Been Sent to

Within a few minutes, you should receive a text message on your phone that includes a verification code. When you receive it, enter it below the text message, try sending it again, or see the App Engine FAQ.

Enter Account Code:

Send

Figure 11-3: Authentication Code screen

application" screen as in figure 11-4. As you can tell I tried to name my application sweeneytest and this was already in use. (What you don't see is that there was already a jimtest, too). Finally, an application identifier of sweeneybooktest worked just fine! I continued by providing my Application Title and agreeing to the legal terms and I was ready to rock and roll!

By clicking on the "Create Application" button, I was then shown the screen in figure 11-5. I was then ready to upload my application and monitor it using the provided dashboard.

Google app engine

Create an Application

You have 10 applications remaining.

Application Identifier:

| sweeneybooktest | .appspot.com | Check Availability | **Sorry, "sweeneytest" is not available.** |

All Google account names and certain offensive or trademarked names may not be used as Application Identifiers.
You can map this application to your own domain later. Learn more

Application Title:

Displayed when users access your application.

Authentication Options (Advanced):   Learn more
Google App Engine provides an API for authenticating your users, including **Google Accounts**, **Google Apps** , and **OpenID** If you choose to use this feature for some parts of you'll need to specify now what type of users can sign in to your application:

Open to all Google Accounts users (default)
If your application uses authentication, anyone with a valid Google Account may sign in.
Edit

Storage Options (Advanced):
Google App Engine datastore options.

High Replication (default)
Uses a more highly replicated Datastore that makes use of a system based on the Paxos algorithm to synchronously replicate data across multiple locations simultaneously. Off highest level of availability for reads and writes, at the cost of higher latency writes, eventual consistency for most queries, and approximately three times the storage and CPU c Master/Slave option. Note: High Replication Datastore is required in order to use the Python 2.7 and Go runtimes.
Edit

Terms of Service:

1. Your Agreement with Google

This License Agreement for Google App Engine (the "Agreement") is made and entered into by and between Google Inc., a Delaware corporation, with offices at 1600 Amphitheatre Parkway, Mountain View 94043 ("Google") and the business entity agreeing to these te ("Customer"). This Agreement is effective as of the date Customer clicks the "I Accept" button below (the "Effective Date"). If you are on behalf of Customer, you represent and warrant that: (i) if you have full legal authority to bind Customer to this Agreement; (ii) you h and understand this Agreement; and (iii) you agree, on behalf of Customer, to this Agreement. If you do not have the legal authority to l

☐ **I accept these terms.**

| Create Application | Cancel |

Figure 11-4: Creating an Application

Google app engine

Application Registered Successfully

The application will use **sweeneybooktest** as an identifier. This identifier belongs in your application's configuration as well. Note that this ident changed. Learn more

The application uses the **High Replication** storage scheme. Learn more

If you use Google authentication for your application, **This is a test for the Book** will be displayed on Sign In pages when users access your a

Choose an option below:

- View the dashboard for This is a test for the Book.
- Use appcfg to upload and deploy your application code.
- Add administrators to collaborate on this application.

Figure 11-5: Application Registered

I then clicked on the "appcfg" button and selected Java as my language. A well-documented web page was then displayed that told me to download the Java SDK and gave me instructions on the several ways that I could upload my Java app to the Google App Engine.

First I needed to download a development environment. Since I selected to demonstrate a Java application, I selected a Java development environment, a tool called "Eclipse™." I downloaded and installed Eclipse™ from the official download site. I selected the "Eclipse IDE for Java Developers" package. I also downloaded and installed the appropriate Java runtime environment which was needed to make Eclipse work. After a few minor installation and configuration issues, probably due to my inexperience with the product, I started Eclipse™ and was presented

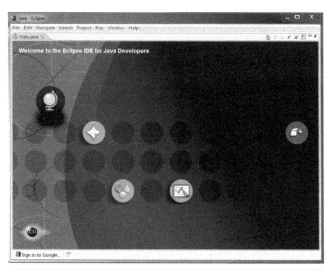

Figure 11-6: The Eclipse IDE for Java Developers

Figure 11-7: Creating a Web Application Project

with the screenshot in figure 11-6.

I then installed the Google Plugin for Eclipse which was just a few steps and in no time at all I was ready to build an application (figure 11-7). I selected my project name (Here I tried "jimtest" again but that actually was in use so I used sweeneybooktest). In a few more mouse clicks I was presented with the development environment (figure 11-8).

Remember, I am not trying to show you how to be a Java programmer, but rather how easy it is to deploy your application in the Cloud!

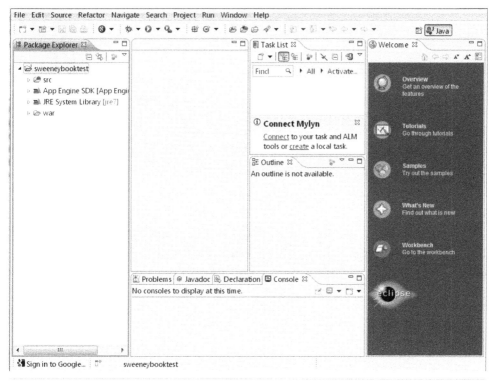

Figure 11-8: My eclipse Project

All I did (in figure 11-9) was click on the Samples button on the right and load a very small Java program, the ubiquitous "Hello World".

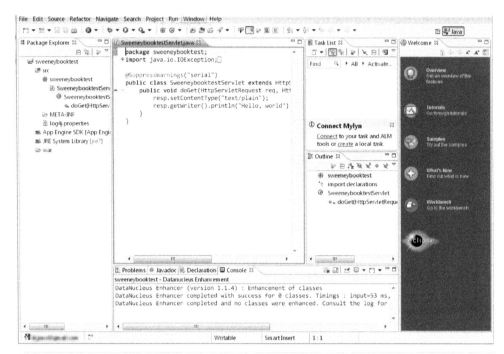

Figure 11-9: Java IDE with sample code loaded

Simply by clicking on the "Run" button in the top of the screen I was running my application (small though it is) in an emulator that is provided with the IDE. The results were displayed in a local browser window as shown in figure 11-10.

I now needed to upload my application to the Google App Engine. Once again that was as easy as a few mouse clicks. As you can see in figure 11-11, this process was started by simply clicking on

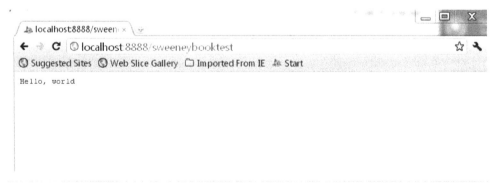

Figure 11-10: Running with the Emulator

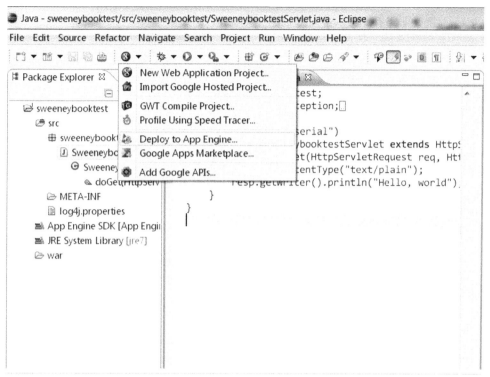

the "G" button (which of course stands for Google) at the top of the screen and then selecting "Deploy to App Engine".

At this point a screen popped up asking me to what project I wished to deploy. Remember sweeneybooktest which was created on the appengine.google.com site just a few mouse clicks ago? I simply inputted that name and hit the "Deploy" button as in figure 11-12.

Figure 11-13 clearly shows that the deployment went smoothly and easily. Please note this is just the "logs" portion of the Eclipse IDE which I enlarged. This screen is normally found in the lower center portion of the environment.

But did it work? By opening a browser and pointing it to sweeneybooktest.appspot.com, you can see (in figure 11-14) that in fact, it did!

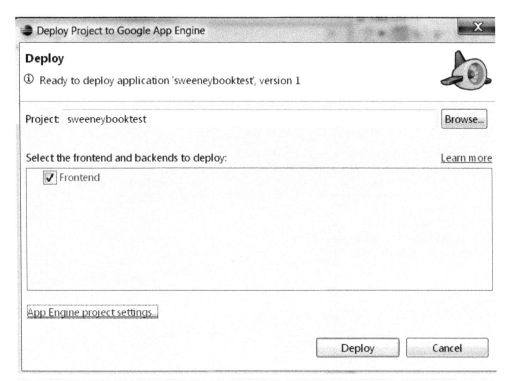

Figure 11-12: Selecting the Project

Figure 11-13: The Log Screen of Eclipse after Deployment

Figure 11-14: It Works!

One thing I really like about the Google App Engine is the documentation. Every step of the way the documentation seems to be consistently great. Not being a real Java developer I was able to follow the steps and get a simple application up and running in very little time with very little effort. I am sure a more robust application would have taken me significantly more time, but for a true Java developer I am sure it would be completed with ease!

CHAPTER
12

PaaS Case Study 1 –
schoolconferences.com

The Agency:
School districts of New Zealand and
the world

Their Challenge:
To develop a cost-effective online system
for scheduling parent-teacher conferences

Their Solution:
A Google App Engine application that
allows parents to schedule conferences
with teachers at times that are convenient
for them

You are a developer. Your children attend local schools. When the principal complains that scheduling parent-teacher conferences is a real hassle and wishes there could be a better way, what do you do?

Greg Fawcett was faced with that very situation. He lives in a very small town in the remote southern part of New Zealand. And the headmaster at his childrens' school asked him to develop a better system. He had already looked into a system to make scheduling these meetings easier but it was quite expensive, especially for a school district of their size.

Greg is a developer who does web development for a number of companies. He realized how powerful a conference scheduling system could potentially be. Using the Google App Engine and its Integrated Development Environment (IDE), Greg wrote a web application for schools to use. Although he is still making improvements to the system, the initial development effort only took about 3 months.

The local school was the first to join. Parents really loved the new system because it made the process of scheduling parent-teacher conferences so much easier. In fact, parents loved it so much that they started talking to their neighbors. Soon, Greg started signing up other schools. Through limited telephone marketing, they signed up even more schools. Most of the growth, however, was viral, coming from word-of-mouth from both parents and school's faculty.

To date, about 25% of the schools in New Zealand use the system. Since all of the larger schools are using schoolconferences.com, approximately 50% of New Zealand school children are covered by this system. The company has recently gone international (The international version is schoolbookings.net). They have schools in the US, Canada, the UK, Italy and most recently, 75 new schools in Australia.

Greg's company was founded in 2009 and is now the "largest in the world at this," according to Greg.

Initially, Greg started off by running his own servers, storage, databases, etc. But "when the thing went down, it was me who was getting up in the middle of the night to go fix things. And if things didn't break, I was still responsible for patching, maintenance, power, cooling and all of that garbage. Now, I don't need to be a system administrator. With Google Apps, I don't need to worry about infrastructure. I just create the product and immediately make it available to the world."

Google App Engine offers the scalability that they need, too. Greg told me, "We don't need to worry about the platform. It just grows along with us. We add a new school and if necessary, Google adds additional resources to satisfy the demand."

Greg interfaces with the Google App Engine using code he wrote in Python. He also uses Google's high replication data store so the master database is online at all times and everything is replicated to a slave database in another data center.

"The beauty of Google App Engine is that I have the best system admins looking out for me. I don't even have to worry about multiple locations in multiple places. It takes about 30 seconds to upload a new version of the software. Google even takes care of replication among the data centers." Greg doesn't know how many servers he is on at any given time, nor does he know or care where those servers are located.

Greg doesn't even worry that Google App Engine is currently hosted from the US. He finds the access times that he and his customers see acceptable for their application.

School Conferences Online is an elegant, but simple-to-use system:

In figure 12-1, we see the well-designed web page that acts as the main landing page for schoolconferences.com. All parents need to know is the "event code" for their school and they can book an appointment. Administrators have previously entered the code and the

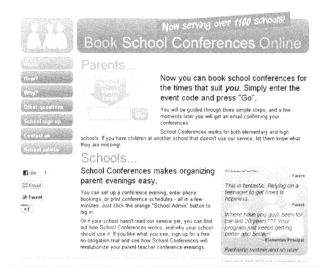

Figure 12-1: Schoolconferences.com

information about the event, including the dates and times that teachers are available to meet. All the parent has to do is log in and pick a time, entering their name and the name of their child.

The "How it works" section (figure 12-2) makes it easy and intuitive for parents to navigate, especially because they will only be using it spo- radically to schedule appointments.

Even the process of signing up a new school is automated and quite simple for non-technical users (figure 12-3).

Figure 12-2: The Booking page

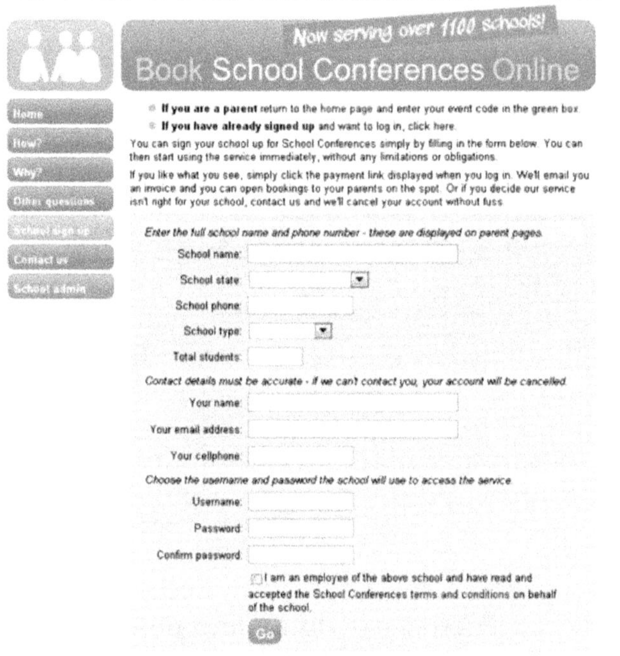

Figure 12-3: School Sign up Page

Greg's company is experiencing double-digit growth every year. To what does he owe his success? "There was a competitor that was charging ten times more than what we charge," said Greg, "But we decided on a different business model. We tried to make a cheaper, one-size-fits all solution." Prices for Greg's service range from $150.00 – $795.00 US dollars per year per school, based upon the total number of students per school.

As they developed and deployed, the biggest problem they faced was one that Greg might not have encountered had he started with Google App Engine in the first place. "Migrating from an in-house database where everything is stored in only one place, to the Google App Engine where data is stored and replicated everywhere, was a real challenge for us," said Greg. "In the Google App Engine, it is nearly impossible to do the same things you do with a SQL database the way you would do them there. The conversion from SQL Database to a Google data store was the key. A complete rethink of the way we were doing things was necessary. It was one of those things that had been drilled into us all through school to always have one copy in one place and we had to totally turn that around."

For others who are considering using the Google App Engine, Greg considers security to be the most important concern. "Schools do in fact have questions about the security of their data. As a consequence, the application stores very little data, just the email addresses of parents. And of course, data like which teachers the parents wish to see but that is not really sensitive information. We really had to think about what data was necessary to store and which was nice to store."

The other concern is control. Compared to AWS or other IaaS systems, you have no control. In other words, you have limited control over where the data resides, and what metrics the Google Cloud uses to determine that another web server is needed. But the converse is peace of mind. "I like to sleep at night," Greg said. "When I use the Google Cloud, I know that if something goes wrong the world's best system administrators are working on it. I couldn't probably do any better, so why shouldn't I let them do it?"

From the website **www.schoolconferences.com**, here are some of the customer comments that Greg has received about his site:

"Everything went fantastically well. I could not imagine going back to the old system."

"One word – Brilliant."

"This is so cool I can't wipe the smile off my face."

School Conference Online is an example of an application developed by an average citizen who saw a need in his community and took action. The result is a great tool for parents and teachers alike, running in the Google Cloud!

PaaS Case Study 2 -

mytowngovernment.org

The Agency:
Town of Barre, Massachusetts

Their Challenge:
Complying with Commonwealth of Massachusetts "Open Meeting" Law that requires all minutes from town boards and committees to be posted online, without the funding to develop a system

Their Solution:
A PaaS Google Apps website that would allow town officials to make public policy information and decisions available to all residents

Suppose you are a small town in Massachusetts and the common-wealth passes an Open Meeting law that requires minutes from all town boards and committees be posted online? The purpose of the law was to ensure transparency in the deliberations upon which public policy is based. Because the democratic process depends on the public knowing about the considerations underly-ing governmental action, the Open Meeting law requires, with some exceptions, that meetings of public bodies be open to the public. It also seeks to balance the public's interest in witnessing the deliberations of public officials with the government's need to manage its operations efficiently.[29]

Cities and communities around the state immediately struggled to meet the requirements of the Open Meeting Law, including:
- 24/7 availability of public meeting postings
- Expanded postings of meetings, including full agendas for all boards and commissions
- Bans on e-mail discussions of issues outside of meetings

In addition, postings must be made 48 hours in advance of a meeting, not including Saturdays, Sundays or holidays. And, meet-ing minutes must include more detailed information, including a list of documents presented and a summary of topics discussed in the meetings.

Communities also had to find a way to retain and archive all records of meetings, including every document, map, photograph or other information used in the meetings, including executive sessions.

Enter Joshua Smith, a town of Barre, MA, Zoning Board of Appeals member with a day job as CTO and cofounder of Kaon Interactive. Working pro bono, Smith created a site that made it easier for the Barre town clerk to comply with the new require-ments, including posting meeting notices and agendas at least 48 hours ahead of time.

29 http://www.mass.gov/ago/government-resources/open-meeting-law/attorney-generals-open-meeting-law-guide.html#Overview

On his website, Joshua says, "As a long-time volunteer on town boards and committees, I know the importance of inter-board communication, and I think making it easier for people to share information is in everyone's best interest. I love the new Open Meeting Law, but I also understand that it comes as a huge 'unfunded mandate' to cities and towns that are struggling to keep their doors open at all."

Josh says that he created **www.mytowngovernment.org** with two objectives in mind:
- To help the town clerk of Barre, MA comply with the new Massachusetts Open Meeting law
- To make it easy for town boards and committees to put their minutes on the town web site

Once he proved that the website was valuable for the town of Barre, Joshua invited other communities to set up sites for themselves. On the My Town Government home page is a link for "Anytown, USA," a tutorial to help other towns create their own local sites. "One of the real problems with the new law was the requirement that meeting notes and other items be available 24/7 to the public," Joshua told me. "Many small towns don't have a building that is open 24/7 to the public."

But Josh didn't stop there. After getting the state Attorney General to bless the new site as meeting the law, he converted an old laptop to an electronic kiosk to allow Town Hall visitors to view meetings and agendas any time the building is open. He took the additional steps of making information available via phone and the town's cable-access programming.

Describing himself as a champion of transparency in government, Smith said he would like to see as many communities as possible take advantage of the site. There is no cost for the service since the town of Barre and the other towns are using only a tiny fraction of the free storage space that Google allows.

But why use the Cloud? One big advantage to using the Google App Engine, Joshua was able to develop 80% of the site in one 2-day weekend. In fact, Joshua says that, "I added some of the frills later and will continue to add functionality. But because we use Google App Engine at work, I already knew the product and coding went as smooth as could be." There were other advantages too. There was no hardware to buy, no co-location fees, and no 3 a.m. panic phone calls when something broke down. He briefly considered an IaaS Cloud, but for this application, he wanted something that was auto-scalable, with everything else handled by the provider. There were no machines to patch, no OS to upgrade, no bandwidth charges, and no load balancers to worry about. They are all taken care of by Google. While using Google App Engine, he realized three powerful things:

- Until they exceed the free quotas that come with the Google App Engine, it won't cost anything to run.

- Thanks to good design decisions he made along the way, Joshua wouldn't have to do anything to handle massive scale. Even if every town in the whole country decided to use this site tomorrow, the system can automatically handle it.

- If something happens at the data center where this site is hosted, Google will immediately dispatch their best and brightest to fix it, and once again, Joshua wouldn't have to do anything. Although the Cloud is not immune to hardware or software problems, when something goes wrong, it will generally be fixed within a couple of hours.

"The whole thing is just a database with some HTML code with CSS, and Javascript. It's really so simple. I just needed something that would work and not need maintenance from me," said Joshua.

If enough communities sign up and use the site for archiving minutes and other documents as well as for posting meeting agendas, he may need to ask towns to contribute $99 a year to help cover the costs of storage in the Google Cloud, etc. However, Joshua said, "since Google has raised their quotas and lowered their prices, I really don't see where we will need to charge local communities for this service anytime soon."

In addition, he says, "The system is designed to be administered by the town clerk. Adding boards, locations, and users is all self-serve, and designed to be very easy to do. When you roll this out in your town, you may want to have someone who can train more computer-timid board clerks on how to enter their meetings into the system, and upload minutes and other documents. In Barre, the town librarian volunteered to be this person."[30]

He also added an interface to the local cable access channel, as well as telephone access, so people could dial in and listen to the minutes of meetings and notices for new meetings.

Using this system, the chairs of boards and committees are now able to post their own notices and agendas. In addition to reducing work for the town clerk's office, the system gives the various board and committee chair people more control over what appears on their agendas. If an agenda item is added after the agenda is posted, the board or committee chair can easily log in and add it. And since the users and administrators can access the site from anywhere, meeting cancellations or changes pose no problems, since they can access the site from home, without having to slog through the inclement New England weather to do it.

In addition, board and committee chairs are instantly notified if they are violating the requirement that postings must be done at least 48 hours in advance. Until last year, only Sundays weren't counted as part of the 48-hour period; new regulations also exempt Saturdays. This means that a meeting scheduled for 7 p.m. on a Monday must be posted by 7 p.m. the previous Thursday.

Josh says, "The feature set of this site will always be a work-in-progress. I'll add features as they are suggested, provided they

---

30 From the mytowngovernment.org website. Used with permission.

are really useful, consistent with Open Meeting and Public Records laws, and do not hurt usability or accessibility for the general public. If you have a feature suggestion, send it to me at the email address on the web site."

Let's take a quick look at the site.

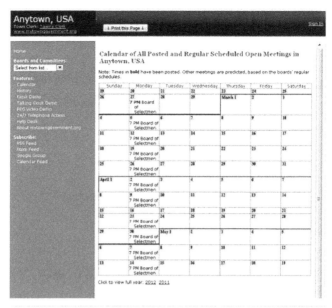

Figure 13-1: The Town Calendar

In figure 13-1, we see a calendar list of current meetings.

The site boasts a complete solution for all of the town's previous meetings so citizens can see the minutes (figure 13-2).

There is also a section of the site (in figure 13-3) that shows what "kiosk mode" looks like. There we find detailed instructions on setting this up for your town.

For those looking to use the site for their town, the site provides a

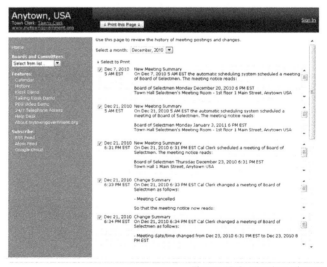

Figure 13-2: Meeting History

sample "roll-out" plan. Because Joshua set this up for use in the Commonwealth of Massachusetts, the site complies with the

Anytown, USA

Open Meetings as of Tuesday February 21, 2012 4:28 PM EST

All meetings before Thursday February 23, 2012 4:28 PM EST must already be posted.

Board	Date	Time	Location	
Board of Selectmen	Mon Feb 27, 2012	7 PM EST	Town Hall	Meeting Room A&B 1st floor
Board of Selectmen	Tue Aug 30, 2050	7 PM EDT		

Stay tuned for details on these meetings...

Figure 13-3: Kiosk mode

Commonwealth's Open Meeting law. Because of the system's flexibility and expandability, however, he stated, "I am happy to work with other towns that have different requirements. I'm sure it wouldn't be a big deal to add their requirements into the system."

In developing My Town Government, Joshua has included a tutorial section (figure 13-4) of the web site that allows users who are not familiar with a digital system to learn in at their own pace. Here are a couple of screenshots of that part of the system:

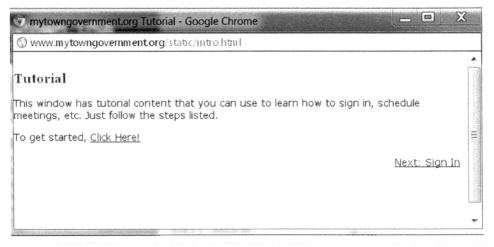

Figure 13-4: The tutorial

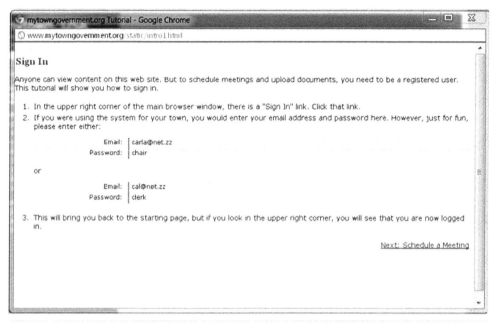

Figure 13-5: Sign In screen

Figure 13-5 shows the sign in screen for the user(s) that are responsible for posting new announcements and meeting minutes.

This simple, yet very functional, website solves a particular problem for local governments within the Commonwealth of Massachusetts. And it's an infinitely scalable web service that was easy to develop and deploy to the PaaS Cloud. It gives the designer, who does not devote full time to this endeavor, the comfort of knowing that the scaling is taken care of automatically, and he doesn't have to worry about hardware, storage, bandwidth, facilities or any of the other aspects that a traditional non-Cloud solution would encompass.

Joshua said that the only real issue for him was the initial learning curve of a PaaS system. "I used Google because that's what we use at work and I already knew it. It's a great system for what I need it to do. But unlike IaaS Clouds, where anyone can get up and running in just a few minutes, you need to know the nuances and the quirks of the development environment of the PaaS provider. True, they hide a lot of the complexities, but there is still a learning curve. The system would have taken me much longer to develop if I hadn't already been intimately familiar with the environment. You really need to immerse yourself and become familiar with the PaaS provider and their tools. Once you do that, you will find all sorts of new uses for the PaaS Cloud."

When I asked Joshua if he had any new projects on the horizon, he told me he was in the middle of three new ones, all developed on the Google App Engine PaaS Cloud, and all of them designed and architected to make life easier for those working in local and community governments.

This is a great example of local government use of the Cloud as well as a great example of a citizen seeing a need then developing the application in the Cloud to solve the problem.

Getting Started with Microsoft Windows Azure

Getting started with the Microsoft Windows Azure™ product is very simple. The first thing you need to get the Windows Azure environment is a Windows Live ID. I didn't have one, but the process was simple and easy, with the usual email verification to prove that the email address I used was actually mine. Then I signed up for a 3 month free trial of Windows Azure, which entailed me giving them the Windows Live UserID that I had just created, getting a text message for verification purposes and providing them a credit card in case I ran over my free allotment of computer hours or storage. The whole process took

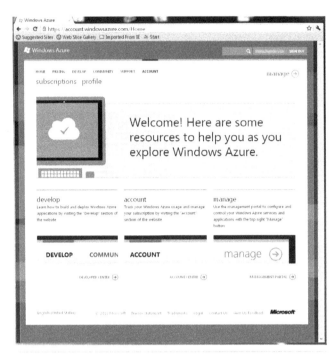

just a few minutes and then I was presented with the welcome screen in figure 14-1.

Of course, now I must decide what language I am going to use to develop my application, then download the appropriate Software Development Kit. I can choose .net, node.js, Java, php, or I can choose a basic SDK that

Figure 14-1: Windows Azure Welcome Screen

will allow me to write my application is just about any language. The first thing I downloaded was Visual Web Developer Express 2010 service pack 1. As it turns out I did not need to download it separately because if you do not have Windows Visual Studio 2010, the SDK automatically downloads and installs it with the Visual Web Develop 2010 Express and the Express version of SQL Server 2008.

After I downloaded what I needed and went through the standard install process, I started up Microsoft Visual Web Developer 2010 Express™ and immediately said I wanted to create a new project from the

Figure 14-2: Starting a new project

ASP.Net MVC 3 Web Application template. (figure 14-2).

Figure 14-3 shows the sample code that was provided as part of the template. All I did was change the html heading to say "Test of Windows Azure for book". Once again, I'm not

Figure 14-3: The modified Sample Code

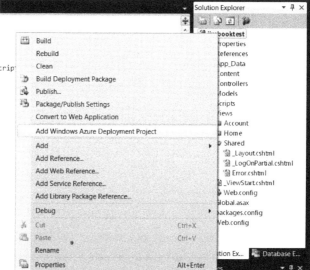

Figure 14-4: Sample Application Test Result

trying to teach you how to code but rather show you how easy it is to create and deploy an application in the Windows Azure Environment.

Running my application locally was now as easy as pressing the F5 button on my keyboard. As you can see from figure 14-4, the sample application worked just fine. You can tell it's running on my local machine because you can see "localhost" in the URL address bar in the figure!

Figure 14-5: Starting the deployment process

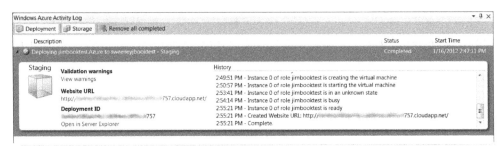

Figure 14-6: The Log screen showing a successful deployment

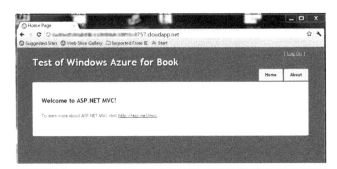

Figure 14-7: Our application works!

Figure 14-8: Back to the management portal for cleanup

Now to deploy! Just like Google, Microsoft makes it easy. With one click (in figure 14-5) I was able to start the deployment process.

And as you can see from figure 14-6, the logs show that the application deployment was successful!

Simply by clicking on the link in figure 14-6, we can see the results (in figure 14-7).

Since I was using part of my free resources that I might want to use for something else, I did take a moment

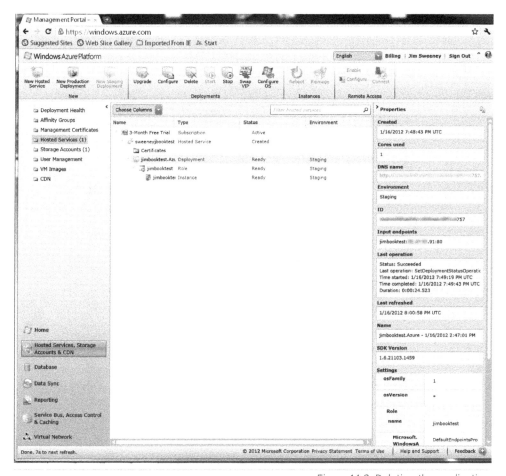

Figure 14-9: Deleting the application

to go through and clean up my application. But again, this was just a few mouse clicks!

By going back to the Windows Azure portal and logging in, I was presented with the screen in figure 14-8. By clicking on the "Hosted Services" in figure 14-9, and then selecting my application and hitting the "delete" key, I was able to quickly and efficiently undo the deployment and free those resources for another time.

After reading this, a friend of mine told me that Amazon had an SDK and should be included in the SaaS section.

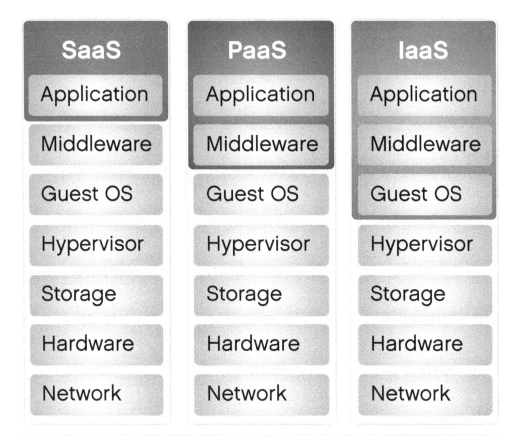

Figure 14-10: A review of the Cloud Service Models

But, while I like the AWS Cloud very much for certain types of workloads, having an SDK does not make you a SaaS Cloud. Remember our diagram? I've repeated it here in figure 14-10.

After I develop in the Google App Engine or the Windows Azure SaaS platform, I upload my application and that is pretty much the end of things. I do not have control over the underlying OS on which the application resides, nor do I have access to change things like the metric that is used to auto-scale up or down. With Amazon, I get those things, but I do not get an emulator on which to test my application locally and a one-button "deploy" function that webifie's and uploads my application without some effort on my part.

Finally, I wanted to take a second to thank my friend Chris Gorski for his help and assistance with this chapter. I am not a developer (the last time I wrote a line of code it was COBOL). It was with his kind help that the material here just seemed to flow. The discussion we had afterwards of the various Cloud providers and when you might use them was also extremely valuable. Chris, I promised you would make it into the book. I doubt great riches will bestow upon you because of it, but I sincerely appreciate your help. You're the best!

CHAPTER 15

PaaS Case Study 3 –

The City of Miami

The Agency:
The City of Miami, Florida

Their Challenge:
Finding a cost-effective, timely way to disseminate information to its nearly half million residents

Their Solution:
A Windows Azure platform that would support and maintain a Web 2.0 application without requiring the purchase of new hardware

The city of Miami occupies approximately 36 square miles of land in southeastern Florida. It offers a tropical climate, beautiful beaches, a dynamic city center, and numerous cultural, historical, and recreational attractions to both its citizens and tourists alike. Its municipal government provides a range of services to more than 425,000 citizens. Although the city's IT department is centralized, the city's 3,600 employees work at 83 sites around the city: fire houses, city municipal buildings, police stations, etc.

Like state and local governments everywhere, the city's IT department was challenged to do more with less. Both IT budgets and staff have been slashed during the latest recession. State and local income taxes fell and the federal government, also facing budget problems, has been unable to assist. The city's IT department did its best to continue to support the current IT infrastructure, maintain the current initiatives, and develop new services for the citizens and visitors of the city.

The budget cuts the city has experienced are dramatic. IT staff has dropped from 104 to 80 in 2010, and currently sits at 64. Their budgets have followed the same trend, dropping 18% one year, and continue to be cut. James Osteen, the former Assistant IT Director for the City of Miami said, "The first things that get cut in any economic downturn are: number 1, training, and number 2, capital expenditures." Miami was hit especially hard since much of its income is derived from tourism, also down significantly during the recent financially-troubling times. These constraints were mirrored at the city level. Because the city was asked to cut another 10% of its operating budget, the IT department has seen a sharp increase in the number of requests it has received to deliver new services.

One key service that the city provides is the 3-1-1 non-emergency phone line used to record and track issues reported by citizens. Just by dialing 3-1-1, residents can report a wide range of issues: potholes, incidents of illegal dumping, missed garbage collection, and more. When they call, residents are issued a service-request number that they can use to monitor the status of the issue, all the way to full resolution. The city IT department wanted to develop a Web application that would allow citizens to track service requests online using their assigned number, and also see the status of other requests in their local area. The city already had the beginnings of this application in place: they had already converted one of its zoning applications to Bing Maps for Enterprise.

But they faced a very familiar conundrum. Do I buy enough hardware to run my application so that I will always satisfy my citizens, but risk wasting money by over-buying? Or do I underestimate my needs, preserve my budget, but run the risk of potentially being unable to provide services during peak periods? Adding to their dilemma, in their hurricane-prone location, the city had to seriously consider disaster recovery. That means they need twice the hardware to ensure enough server redundancy to keep its infrastructure running in the event of a natural disaster. So what were their options? The IT department needed a solution that could offer enough processing power and storage to host applications with sophisticated mapping technologies. The solution they chose would also need to provide the ability to scale up (and scale down) during peak periods of use, without requiring that they attempt to predict processing power and server load requirements for a five-year period. In addition, they needed a solution that would simplify and increase the application development and deployment processes.

In order to reduce costs, the city had to re-evaluate the way it was doing business and reinvent its IT department. To deliver its 311 application to residents, the city of Miami chose the Windows® Azure platform, along with Bing maps, which takes advantage of sophisticated mapping technology. This was an especially good decision for two reasons:

- This GIS application required significant computing resources, but the city did not have a budget for new hardware. Using some of their existing hardware was out of the question because the city is currently on a 5-year hardware refresh cycle. For the City of Miami this means the IT department can only procure new server hardware once every five years and must predict its server needs for five years in the future. It would be very difficult to predict the requirements for such a system, especially since it hadn't been built yet.

- The development environment for Windows® Azure allowed the developers to run and test an application on their local computer before deploying it. They did not have to use multiple testing, debugging, and production environments before deploying new applications or updates. They were able to deploy the new application faster and less expensively than with traditional methods.

Why did they choose Microsoft? Jim Osteen explained, "First, the city already supports its infrastructure with Microsoft products, including the Microsoft .NET™ Framework 3.5, so we were already familiar with the development environment. Secondly, we chose Windows Azure because the IT department had recently evaluated Microsoft Visual Studio 2010™ development system and was impressed with its seamless integration with the development fabric in Windows Azure. Finally, the city based its decision in part on the pay-as-you-go pricing model for Windows Azure, which was a hit with the department given the budget challenges it faced."

Even more impressive, Windows Azure allowed the city IT department to develop Miami 3-1-1 in eight days with two people. They realized a 75% reduction in development costs, simply by using the Cloud! True, they had some help from ISC, a Microsoft Partner located in Florida. ISC worked with the city to develop the application and integrate it with their existing database and application development efforts.

Osteen continued, "In addition to the fast development, we were able to reduce costs. With Windows Azure, we can scale horizontally and vertically very quickly as demand requires, without worrying about predicting our server needs five years in advance. Also, by relying on Microsoft-hosted data centers, we've improved our disaster-recovery strategy, which is important in our hurricane-prone region."

"Miami was the first to implement our solution," says Benton Belcher, Business Development Manager for ISC. "After the success of that project, we 'product-ized' the offering and now officials from as far away as Georgia and California are using a similar system. County commissioners and city officials really like that they have transparency to see everything happening in the district or region."

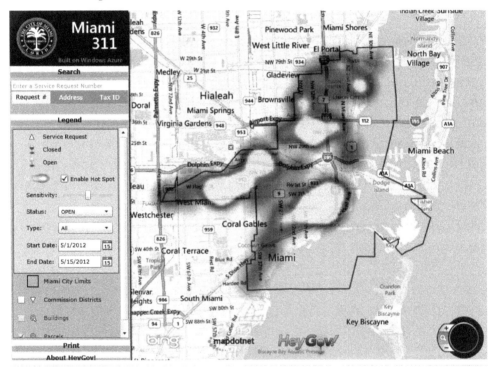

Figure 15-1: The Miami 311 Application

With Microsoft Windows Azure the city is now able to bring new applications online more quickly and has improved its ability to offer new, enhanced services to Miami residents while reducing costs. By relying on hosting at Microsoft data centers, the hurricane-prone city has greatly improved its disaster-recovery strategy. In fact, immediately after launching the application, the city decided to add features to enhance the product, including the ability for users to submit service requests with photos, and to send a description directly from their Windows phone or Apple iPhone®. In addition, the city could send status updates and notifications by e-mail or text message back to the user.

As you can see in figure 15-1, citizens of Miami can now view a myriad of data all in one place. I have turned on commissioner districts (the gray areas) and am showing the "Hot Spots," which in this case show the concentrated groups of reports of illegal dumping. According to Benton, "The city wanted a modern Web 2.0 application. Now anyone with a web browser can get involved in their community."

Osteen agrees, "With Microsoft Windows Azure, we're relying on a trustworthy solution—everything is hosted at Microsoft in data centers in multiple geographic locations—to make things simpler for our organization. We don't have to worry about managing a costly infrastructure and can focus on delivering new services that positively impact citizens and our organization."

Even with their tight IT budget, the city of Miami can run a lean IT department and rely on Microsoft to manage the IT infrastructure for this application. Windows Azure allows the city to eliminate much of its need to procure, host, and manage its own physical servers—representing a 75% savings to the city. "Using the Microsoft Windows Azure product allowed us to switch from capital budget to operating budget dollars. But that wasn't all. It also saved us a considerable amount of time. Ordering a server on the state contract would take us up to 3 months. Then I had to have our people rack and stack the machine and worry about uptime and things like that. Now our folks can move up the stack and worry about higher-end problems. We know that Microsoft takes care of the infrastructure."

What about disaster recovery? The city spends about 3 months out of every year preparing and testing for hurricane season. Osteen said, "Now we don't have to worry about Mother Nature. Even if one of the Microsoft data centers was taken out, they have the full redundancy and backup that we need to keep going."

The city of Miami has experienced no downtime since they put this system in place 3 years ago. They are currently looking at moving 4 or 5 applications off their aging mainframe computer and into the Cloud to save even more money!

After the success of the Miami 3-1-1 project, James Osteen left city government and is now the Executive Director of the Broadband Coalition. One of the many things that this organization does is help local governments move to Office 365, then take the savings they realize from not having their own Exchange servers and licenses, and put that money back into training people to cross the digital divide! In his new role, James is using what he learned about Cloud to educate others in the latest technology.

16

Private IaaS Clouds, Hybrid Clouds and Community Clouds

In this chapter we'll examine Private Infrastructure-as-a-Service Clouds, Community Clouds and Hybrid Clouds. The basic model for this type of Cloud is seen in figure 16-1.

While Private Clouds are now being treated as the scourge of the government by some people in the public sector and industry-at-large, they do have their place. And while you can have an Private Cloud that is an SaaS Cloud or a PaaS Cloud, by far the most popular is the IaaS Private Cloud, so that is the one we'll discuss here. The IaaS private Cloud also leads nicely into the Hybrid Cloud.

Hybrid Clouds are a mixture of a Private Cloud combined with the flexibility and elasticity of a Public Cloud. VMware's vCloud product is the most advanced technology used for creating IaaS Clouds internally and, not surprisingly, the most popular for creating the Hybrid Cloud. Terremark has implemented the VMware vCloud technology and is already accepting federal, state, and local customers.

Community Clouds are a favorite in the federal government where many agencies must come together for a short period of time, for example, in a natural disaster. We'll investigate some of these instances and talk about their advantages and disadvantages.

Figure 16-1: The IaaS Cloud Model

Private Clouds

I am not a fan of Private Clouds, but there are some legitimate reasons to use them, such as:

1. One of the basic tenets of Cloud is the ability to pay only when you use a resource and correspondingly, not pay for it when you don't. A Private Cloud violates this rule because there are capital expenditures up front. I would never recommend buying servers, storage, and networking gear in order to build a private IaaS Cloud, but what if you already have the infrastructure in place? If you simply want to offer IaaS services to your customers, you could create a Private Cloud with a small investment to enable self-service provisioning. Over time, you could possibly transition to a Hybrid Cloud.

2. By definition, a Private Cloud doesn't meet the elasticity

requirements for Cloud. In other words, growing and shrinking your usage as business conditions dictate. But this argument only holds so much water. Take the Terremark or Amazon IaaS Cloud offerings, for example. While it is true that you could scale your application (workloads) up and down as business needs dictate, in reality, you can...and you can't. Both of these providers, while excellent, only scale so far. Could you add 1 new CPU today if you needed? I would almost guarantee it. 10? Sure. 100? Yes, I'll give you that. How about a thousand? Ten thousand? Or even a million CPUs? Somehow I think that might tax even their well-designed systems.

There is a real-world reason, however, to provision this many workloads: high performance computing (HPC). Those folks are breaking up discrete workloads into hundreds, or thousands, or tens or even hundreds of thousands of discrete tasks. There are several HPC clusters running today with multiple thousands of compute nodes all spinning along and computing very nicely. So once again, the argument that a Private Cloud is not elastic is true as long as you don't get too crazy in your thinking. But the same could be said of your architecture. Your virtualized servers, with network connections and some kind of storage attached may be able to scale up and down in the 1-, 5-, and 10-CPU range – just not in the 1,000+ range like a Public Cloud provider. You do have some measure of elasticity in your Private Cloud. It's just not the same range of scalability that a public provider would support.

3. An IaaS Cloud provider has all the management tools built in. On the surface, that is true. But for a modest sum of money, and some modifications, you can add management tools to your existing infrastructure, creating a basic IaaS Cloud solution that your customers can use to provision new workloads. It might not be as robust as a custom-built management solution, but it's workable and cost-effective.

How is a Private Cloud built and what are some of their components? Agencies first looked at physical Infrastructure-as-a-Service (IaaS) Clouds in an effort to save money and increase services to their constituents. Even VMware is starting their Cloud offerings with an architecture that is designated as IaaS.

The key characteristics of a Private IaaS Cloud to consider are:
- The ability to dynamically scale and provision computing power in a cost-efficient way using a virtualized environment within a common redundant physical infrastructure. (You cannot have a true Cloud environment that all resides completely in one data center or location.)
- The ability of the consumer to use a self-service portal to make the most of that power without having to manage the underlying complexity of the technology.
- The ability to accurately charge the consumer for services requested and delivered.
- The network security to ensure that multiple tenants only have access to their environment and not anyone else's.

Since one of the foundations of Cloud computing is a virtualized infrastructure, let's begin with server virtualization. This subject needs almost no introduction, but for the uninitiated, we'll look at the server virtualization product from VMware, then introduce the features of their newest offering, called a Cloud Computing System.

VI3 and vSphere

VMware® and their **Virtual Infrastructure 3** was the first generation of server virtualization to gain industry-wide acceptance. Because of its reliability, and the number of built-in features, Virtual Infrastructure 3 quickly became the gold standard for virtualizing servers. It was the first product that reliably and consistently allowed multiple virtual servers (VMs) and their applications to run unmodified on off-the-shelf physical hardware. While there are several non-x86 vendors offering Cloud, most people are looking at x86 workloads, so we will focus on that.

VI3, as it was commonly called, had a number of important building blocks that made it so popular:
- vMotion – The ability to manually move a running virtual machine from one physical server to another without disrupting the users connected to that virtual machine.
- Dynamic Resource Schedule (DRS) – An automatic (or manual) feature that allows VMware to move virtual machines around a cluster of physical machines as needed to gain maximum use of resources across all the virtual machines.
- High Availability (HA) – Allows VI3 to automatically restart virtual machines that are no longer running due to failure of an underlying physical machine.

Their newest offering, **vSphere**, is not billed as a virtualization platform, but rather a "Cloud Computing" platform. Regardless, there are a number of impressive new features in vSphere that move current users to consider upgrading. Some of vSphere's upgraded benefits include:

Scale Up

The resource limits for both virtual and physical machines have been greatly expanded. Virtual machines can now have up to 32 virtual CPUs (increased from 8) and up to 1 TB of RAM (previously 255 GB). The underlying physical hardware can scale to 2 TB of RAM and 128 total cores! This means you can now run many more virtual machines on fewer, but larger, physical machines, making data center management a bit easier. It also means you can now run workloads that you may have thought previously were too large for a virtualized environment.

In addition, it is now possible to "hot add" both CPU and memory to your virtual machines. You cannot, however, "hot delete" these same features. Taking away memory or CPUs while an application is running can have disastrous results and is not permitted. You can however, "hot add" and "hot remove" both storage and network devices. These features are a wonderful addition to the product line.

vStorage Thin Provisioning

When you create your virtual machines and specify the hard disk size, there is an option for thin provisioning. When setting up the vSphere cluster in our lab, the engineers at GTSI tried this feature and it truly works as advertised. We set up a test virtual machine and gave it a 60GB disk drive, but checked the option to thin provision it. After installing the OS, there was an 8GB hard disk there! As we add additional software to that virtual machine, the size increases as we need it. This feature is independent of any thin provisioning that you may do at the LUN level of your storage. One word of caution: as with any thin-provision technology, over-provisioning means that you will need to pay closer attention to your storage to avoid running out! It is a VERY bad idea to use thin-provisioning at the server layer and also use thin-provisioning at the storage layer. This is double trouble just waiting to happen.

Fault Tolerance (FT)

In VI3, we had High Availabilty (HA), the ability to restart virtual machines that are no longer running when the physical machines fail. HA is a good feature, but it has one big disadvantage: there is a short outage while the virtual machines from the failed host are restarted. What if you cannot afford even a short outage? Enter Fault Tolerance. With Fault Tolerance, an identical virtual machine runs in lockstep with the original, but is running on a separate host. To the external world, they appear as one instance (one IP address, one MAC address, one application), but in reality, they are fully redundant instances of virtual machines. If an unexpected hardware failure occurs that causes the active (i.e., primary) virtual machine to fail, a second, (i.e., passive) virtual machine immediately picks up and continues to run, uninterrupted, without any loss of network connections or transactions. Because this technology works at a layer underneath the operating system and application, it can be used on any OS and on any application that is supported by VMware without modification.

Virtual Distributed Switch (VDS)

Perhaps the greatest feature of vSphere is the Virtual Distributed Switch. In VI3, each host had its own series of virtual switches containing all of the network characteristics of all of the virtual machines on that host. It was – and is – a very powerful feature that offers very granular control over the networking character-istics of the cluster. Unfortunately, that was also the downside of this feature. Network engineers hated the fact that certain aspects of the network were now in the hands, and under the control of the server/storage managers. Horror stories abound about network problems caused by improper configuration of the virtual switches. vSphere still has this capability, but has added the capability to support a Virtual Distributed Switch. This allows for even more granular control (for example, monitoring traffic be-tween virtual machines on the same physical server), while giving network administrators control over the network and the server administrators control over the servers. Now our network is truly Cloud-ready!

Features such as these have established VMware as the current leader in this marketplace.

VMware and the Private Cloud

So if we already have a VMware-virtualized environment, what would we need to take a virtualized infrastructure and make it an IaaS Cloud infrastructure? Assuming that vSphere provides the "ability to dynamically scale and provision computing power in a cost efficient way using a virtualized environment within a com-mon redundant physical infrastructure," what more do we need? Following GTSI's Cloud Maturity Model (Appendix C), developed by Prem Jadhwani, the first step is creating some kind of self-service portal.

vCloud Director

The vCloud Director has three very important and far-ranging jobs to do:

1. Act as the overall Cloud Coordinator talking to vSphere and (through vCenter) controlling the creation of virtual machines.

2. Act as the portal where users come to request new virtual machines. The user can choose characteristics of their virtual machine: number of processors, amount of RAM, size of disk, which pre-built template to deploy, other software to add to the template, etc.

3. Function as the Administrator portal where Cloud Managers set up templates, load software packages, develop approval workflows (using an add-on product from VMware called vCloud Request Manager), create and manage user groups, allowing them to have access to virtual machines of various sizes and lengths of times with certain templates, etc.

4. Function as the "glue" tying discrete locations (vCloud cells) together into one Cloud.

VMware vCloud Director also has built-in logical constructs to facilitate a secure multi-tenant environment, if users require it.

Other vendors have similar offerings that are very good in their own right. Computer Associates has a product called CA Automation Suite for Cloud™. It performs the same functions as vCloud Director, but has the ability to provision both virtual and bare metal physical machines as well (Cisco UCS blades, for example). BMC also is a strong competitor in this section of the marketplace; and server OEM's (Cisco, HP, IBM, and Oracle) are getting into the game too. So there are several vendors with strong offerings from which to choose.

vCenter Chargeback

Moving to the next phase in our Cloud Maturity Model, it's time to add the ability to charge users for the resources that they use. vCenter Chargeback meters usage and provides reporting to allow for individual charge-back or show-back to users. Administrators can set up charges for:

1. Product licensing – Fixed cost charges for each Microsoft OS license used on the virtual machine

2. Usage – Actual CPU, memory, network, and storage usage can be separately monitored and charged

3. Administrative Fees – A per-virtual machine fee can be set up for administrative overhead

While we reference the VMware product, companies like Computer Associates, BMC and others have built chargeback into their Cloud Provisioning and Management software. There are also smaller companies that specialize in the charge-back/show-back aspect of Cloud, giving you several options from which to choose.

We now have created a flexible infrastructure with a portal for users and we can charge them correctly for the resources they use. It's time to add security to the mix!

VMware vShield

vCloud Director is designed for secure multi-tenancy so that multiple organizations do not impact one another. For securing user access, the product ships with the built-in LDAP/Active-Directory integration. In addition, user access and privileges within vCloud Director are controlled through role-based access control (RBAC). There are additional steps that can be taken to harden the environment.

vShield provides all of the important pieces of network security, including:

1. vShield Firewall – Used when configuring access to the virtual machines

2. vShield Edge Virtual Appliances – Built-in devices deployed

automatically by vCloud to facilitate routed network connections using 3 different methods, including MAC encapsulation

In addition, vShield features a built-in management console called vShield Manager.

vCloud API

vCloud API is a set of programming tools, application programmer interfaces and constructs around which the user can make their applications "Cloud-aware." Developers can now build in "Cloud-awareness" into their applications, making it easier to design, deploy and manage applications within a Cloud environment.

The Architecture

What would a good Private IaaS Cloud architecture look like? In the GTSI Lab, we have set up a representative Private IaaS Cloud simulating two data centers or Cloud-nodes. In figure 16-2 you can see it looks like this:

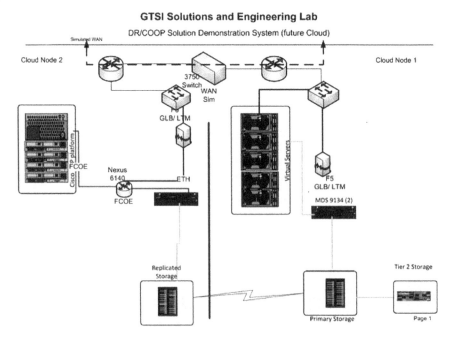

Figure 16-2: GTSI IaaS Private Cloud

On the right is a vDC (vCloud Data Center) node, called Cloud Node 1. On the left side, there is another vDC node, called Cloud Node 2. The vCloud Director, vChargeback and vShield are all implemented in virtual machines.

Besides the server and storage hardware, we use F5 Big IP Global Load Balancers. Present at each site, these devices constantly communicate with each other to perform essentially two functions:
1. Determine to which site to send the user traffic, based on proximity to the requester
2. Determine whether either vDC node is down and, if so send all traffic to the other site

We have replicated storage in real-time between the sites. This is one significant reason why some previous private Cloud implementations have failed. Underestimating the size of this link leads to user dissatisfaction and overall system failure in numerous ways. For example, users connected to one Cloud-node expect to reconnect automatically to another Cloud node if the first Cloud goes down. They expect to see what they were working on a second ago, not what they were working on 24 hours ago.

I really like the vCloud product and adding it to your already-virtualized infrastructure is a great way to start down the road to Private and then Hybrid Cloud.

Now let's take a look at an alternative to VMware from CA Technologies®.

The CA Private IaaS Cloud Offering

CA Technologies offers an alternative to the Cloud management layer from VMware. In fact CA has two viable solutions for agencies that want to set up Private, Hybrid or Community Clouds. We'll explore both offerings, and identify differences between the two solutions.

There are many vendors in this space competing with VMware. CA is certainly not the only one. Among others, HP has their BTO suite, IBM has their Tivoli product line, and BMC has a mature and well-thought-out offering.

CA Automation for Clouds™

The CA Automation Suite for Clouds was formerly known as Spectrum Automation Manager. It provides a self-service portal and service catalog with native multi-tenancy already built in. It also includes pre-configured, automated workflows and service definitions. If your users are going to be able to go to a portal and choose a 2 processor virtual machine with 2 GB of RAM and a Windows 2008 64 bit OS with SQL Server, as the system administrator, you must:

1. Create templates, patch them, and keep them up to date with all of the software and tools that your agency requires
2. Set up users and groups, determining what privileges each group will need
3. Establish automated workflow procedures that kick in when users do things like:
   a. Request more machines than they are allotted
   b. Request bigger machines than they are allotted
   c. Let machines expire

CA Technologies treats the Private Cloud as a piece of infrastructure that must be managed as part of the enterprise. Once you get to this stage, this is no longer the Virtualization-Cluster-In-the-Corner that some daring soul managed to establish. It is now part of your enterprise architecture and needs to be managed as such. For a Private IaaS Cloud, the CA Automation Suite for Clouds also includes:

- Service metering and billing to support fixed or usage-based pricing, a billing and financial reporting engine, and integrated chargeback

- Dynamic resource and workload management that can be dynamically scaled up and down to supports shared, pooled resources

- Flexible on-demand provisioning including policy-based automation across physical, virtual and Cloud environments. This is in contrast to VMware's vCloud Director™ which is primarily focused on the virtual side of things. Since you may have some workloads that may not be virtualized at this point, why not use one tool to manage your entire environment?

- Automated discovery, configuration and compliance management to streamline and simplify resource-intensive, error-prone configuration and compliance management processes

The CA Automation Suite for Clouds also interfaces with several other solutions that are worth mentioning:

- **Infrastructure Management** – Now that you have an infrastructure on which you are offering your customers guaranteed SLAs, it's important to manage this infrastructure appropriately. It is no longer enough to manage this cluster like you have in the past by letting VMware restart the virtual machines on a hardware server failure but not automatically putting in a trouble ticket to fix the underlying hardware. This is now a critical piece of your agency's infrastructure and it needs to be managed as such. It provides three critical functions:

  - Discovering infrastructure and mapping and dynamically maintaining relationships between the various pieces of the infrastructure

  - Standardizing management and triage across physical and virtual servers, in both your Private and Public Clouds

  - Optimizing system behavior to predict end-user problems before they occur

- **Service Operations** – You must improve the quality of the IT services you are providing to your customers while lowering your support costs to provide them. Once again, this encompasses three critical aspects of service operation:

- Correlating data from 3rd party tools for real-time, end-to-end service models. If you have various tools managing service, this tool collects data from the tools you already own and correlates them to provide an accurate picture of the health of that service.
- Analyzing how components from various technology silos in your organization are currently impacting service or how they may impact service in the future
- Pinpointing root causes and mitigating risk across traditional and hybrid environments.
- **Application Performance** – It is no longer enough to migrate an application to the Cloud and hope that it is performing correctly. In order to properly account for all performance aspects of any application, this function provides three essential reporting functions:
  - Delivering end-to-end transaction visibility across physical, virtual, and Cloud. Let's say your web servers are in the Cloud, but your database is not yet virtualized. You can't manage these separately, but rather need to manage the total performance of the complete application.
  - Linking the end-user experience with business impact to prioritize problem resolution.
  - Accelerating triage and root-cause diagnostics when problems occur. Case in point: I was with a customer about a year ago. They had several hundred virtual machines up and running on an infrastructure designed for about 50 virtual machines. They started to get flooded with calls from users complaining about performance but had no idea where to look. All they had were the standard VMware tools which were only telling them about the performance of the cluster, but not a lot about application performance. I was shocked to hear them tell their users, "Just wait a few minutes and it will work itself out. It usually does this overnight, so it may not be until tomorrow that things are back to normal for you." Obviously this is not and should not be acceptable to you or your users.

At GTSI, we like the CA system for its ease of use and flexibility. All of our engineers use this tool to request resources from our lab. It makes our job as administrators easier and helps us keep track of what virtual machines a particular user is using, and for how long.

CA AppLogic™

Another offering from CA is called CA AppLogic. CA Applogic is a turnkey Cloud computing platform for composing, running and scaling distributed applications. AppLogic operates on the logical structure of the application, enabling you to package an entire multi-tier application into a logical entity and manage it as a single system. This approach also makes it very easy to assemble, deploy, monitor, control and troubleshoot applications visually in a browser.

Setting it up on your existing infrastructure is easy. A CA AppLogic-powered Cloud consists of two or more servers con-nected via a gigabit Ethernet network to form the grid. Each server has two Ethernet ports. One gigabit port is connected to the network that forms the server grid backbone. The second port is connected to the rest of the data center and out to the public Internet. This architecture allows CA to keep the backbone network private and secure while it provides non-blocking gigabit connectivity between the physical hosts.

A standard CA AppLogic software image is installed on each serv-er before adding it to the "Cloud." Part of each physical server is designated as a controller and runs the management portion of the system. The Cloud operator manages the Cloud by accessing the controller through a secure browser connection. AppLogic uses the hard disks of the physical servers to create a shared, mirrored storage pool called the integrated IP SAN. Because CA AppLogic doesn't require a shared storage system like a SAN or NAS, it's great for smaller department Private Clouds.

What are the real differences? The Data Center Automation Suite for Cloud is using hardware on which you are already running a hypervisor (such as VMware) so your hardware must meet their specifications. Conversely, the AppLogic system includes its own hypervisor, which means you don't have to have one when you start out, or it can make use of your existing Xen or VMware hypervisor. However, the AppLogic system does take over your entire infrastructure. So if you wish to use your Private Cloud for something other than an IaaS Cloud, then the AppLogic system may not be a great solution for you. On the other hand, the AppLogic system is simple to install, easy to use and very easy to learn. Many users are up and running with generic hardware and no shared storage in just a few hours. Where the AppLogic system really shines is situations where you have multiple data centers around the globe. One small set of "Platform Architects" could develop applications and solution sets which users around the world could instantly select and run. This is illustrated in figure 16-3 where centrally located platform architects define

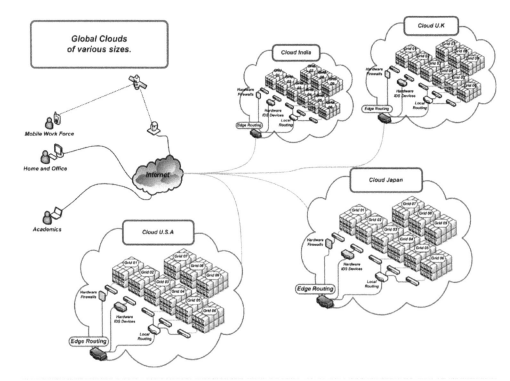

Figure 16-3: AppLogic in a Multiple Data Center Environment

services and make them available to various Cloud cells around the world. Since it runs on just about any generic x86 hardware and many types of SAN and NAS storage devices, it's ideally suited for use in environments that are spread out around the globe which may or may not possess the same hardware.

Hybrid Clouds

Although Private Clouds have often been used as an excuse for not conducting a thorough review of Cloud types and determining which one is most appropriate, they do have their place. There are many competitors to the CA family of products, but the solution set they provide offers many advantages.

Hybrid Clouds are more interesting from the standpoint of where things are going rather than where they are today. In a Hybrid Cloud, you generally have a Private IaaS Cloud, but you also have some of the same constructs set up in a Public Cloud. You can put workloads in either place or move them from one place to another (Public to Private or Private to Public). Currently, in order to move them back and forth, we must shut workloads down; very soon, that may not be the case. In the future, you will be able to move entire "vApps" around from several internal and external Clouds just as easily as you use the vMotion ability to migrate virtual machines from one physical server to another today. In fact, we may well have a Cloud version of Dynamic Resource Scheduler (DRS) that moves vApps automatically from one Cloud to another (within limits of course) as utilization and resource requirements dictate.

Again, VMware with their vCloud offering is one of the leaders in this area. You can purchase Public Cloud services from Terremark that are built using vCloud constructs. You can set your Private Cloud to be part of a Hybrid Cloud with the Public vCloud offering from Terremark. Hybrid Clouds allow you to easily manage your resources and move entire vApps around from internal to external and back as required. Here are a couple of potential scenarios:

1. **Scenario #1:** You have everything running in your data center

as a Private Cloud and are satisfied with the way everything is performing. But all of a sudden, a new requirement crops up from the developers and they need more resources than you can provide on your already-stretched-too-thin infrastructure. You could set the developers and their virtual machines up in the external Cloud (using something like vCloud). Then, when budget cycles allow you to get more hardware or business needs ebb, you could move the entire set of virtual machines back to your Private Cloud.

2. **Scenario #2:** Perhaps it's not a technology decision at all. Maybe Terremark's service is cheaper than you can provide internally. With a Hybrid Cloud set up between the two Cloud cells (one cell at Terremark's facility and one at your own), you can now decide which vApps to send where, based on cost of storage, processor, or bandwidth at that particular moment.

Hybrid Clouds are the way to go for most agencies. Not for all services or applications, of course. For email, you may choose a public SaaS model. Or maybe you want to put collaboration on an Private SaaS Cloud with Sonian. For those considering private IaaS Clouds, Hybrid is only a couple of steps away from Private, yet you get the flexibility and rapid expandability not possible with a Private Cloud. With Hybrid Clouds you get the best of both worlds: the Private Cloud for very secure workloads and the Public Cloud for less-sensitive workloads that may need to rapidly expand and contract. What's more, you can manage them all as one all-encompassing agency-wide infrastructure, rather than running management tools from different vendors.

The vCloud product from VMware allows you to set up a Private Cloud, and then quickly and easily connect with the vCloud running at Terremark. So you can be up and running in no time. The Terremark offering is a powerful set of tools for running your agency when used in combination with a Private Cloud running VMware.

Another option for implementing Hybrid Clouds is the CA Automation Suite for Clouds. It can support both Private and Public Clouds, and it will manage both virtual and physical hardware so you can use one suite of products to manage your entire infrastructure. You can actually integrate all three products, depending on your specific requirements. You could employ vCloud for moving workloads around, the CA AppLogic suite for creating solutions, and the CA Automation Suite for Clouds to manage the environment.

The Community Cloud

There is a lot of confusion surrounding Community Clouds. Community Clouds are Clouds (private, public, or hybrid) that are shared across people having the same interests. For example, the Intelligence agencies of the US may need to share a common data base of persons-of-interest and could all access the same SaaS Hyperoffice Suite in order to share contacts, program schedules, etc.

Or every agency that deals with GIS data could share a Cloud that hosts all of the known GIS data in the US as well as the various applications for using and manipulating that data.

In this era of budget cuts, Community Clouds may prove to be an effective tool for sharing information, resources, and applications among a set of users with common interests.

17

Getting Started with vCloud

Provisioning in a vCloud system is very complete. A few of the main screens from the vCloud cell in our lab will show you the basic functionality of the vCloud system. Figure 17-1 shows the very simple, but functional, login screen.

Once you have logged in with administrator privileges, you will see the administration screen (figure 17-2) with 3 main tabs. The first tab is the home screen. This is where you add another vCenter (or Private Cloud node), another provider vDC, manage the organization and system administrators, and manage the resources assigned to each.

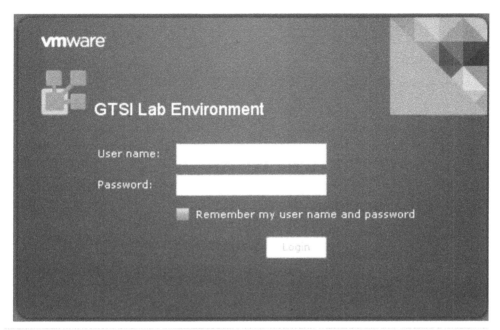

Figure 17-1: The vCloud Login Screen

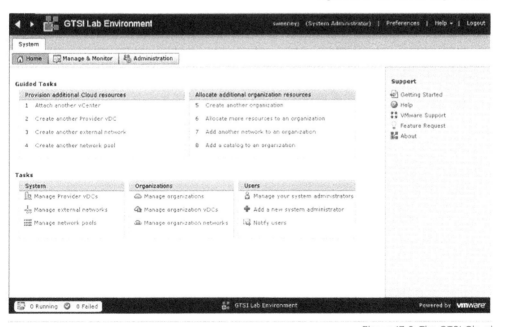

Figure 17-2: The GTSI Cloud

In figure 17-3 we see the second tab which is the administration tab, where you manage the system settings, such as LDAP integration, email servers, licensing, etc. (The identity of our site administrators has been grayed-out for privacy.)

Figure 17-3: Administration Tab

Figure 17-4: The Manage and Monitor Tab

The third tab is the management and monitoring screen. Once you are set up with the basics on the home and administration screens, this is where most of the work is done. On this screen, I can manage my organizations, in our case: CloudSolutions,

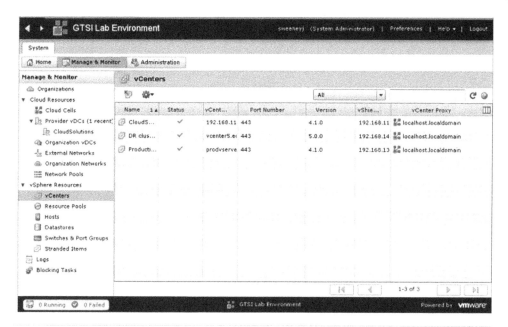

Figure 17-5: The GTSI vCenters

Finance and HR. They are all enabled and connected to one vDC, and they each have one user (figure 17-4).

To look at the VMware vCenter management consoles attached to my environment, I click on the "vCenters" button. There are three vCenters connected to our vCloud cell in figure 17-5.

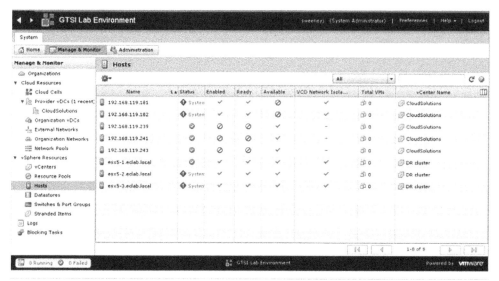

Figure 17-6: GTSI hosts

We can also look at the individual hosts that make up our environment. As you can see from figure 17-6, it appears that we have a few hosts with some problems! This screen allows you to immediately identify the problems within your Cloud environment!

(In reality, these are Cisco UCS chassis blades that get repurposed for other things, and then are converted back to VMware ESXi hosts as we need them, so there really is no problem in our lab, but it did serve as a nice example.)

We can also take a look at the data stores (figure 17-7) that are a part of our environment.

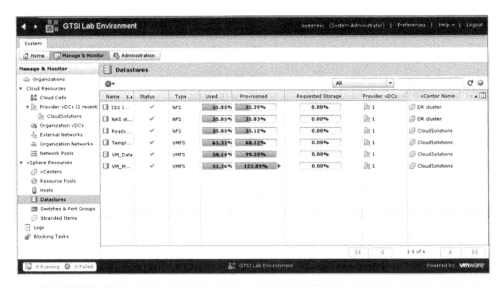

Figure 17-7: GTSI Datastores

There are several storage pools available to us. One of them, the last one, is over-provisioned using the thin provisioning feature of VMware. All in all, you can see that the VMware vCloud interface is easy to use and provides a complete picture of your Private Cloud environment.

Getting Started with CA

The service creation process is really quite simple. Since there are two ways to create services with CA we will examine them both starting with the CA Automation Suite for Clouds.

CA Automation Suite for Clouds – The User's screens

Let's start with the user's screenshots. The CA Automation Suite for Cloud makes it very simple to provision all kinds of virtual or even physical machines in an easy-to-use template manner. We'll start from the beginning and review the process necessary to request a server. In figure 18-1, we see the login screen that is presented to the user.

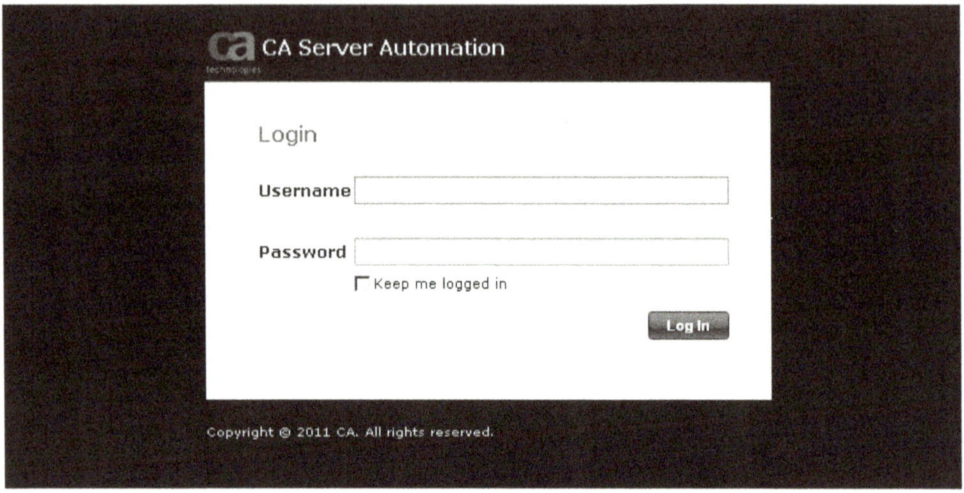

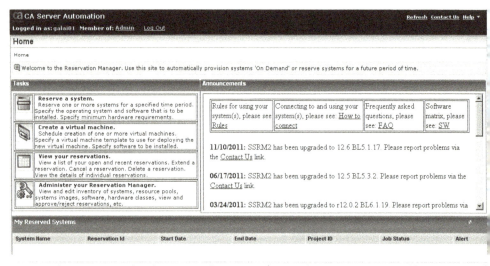

Figure 18-1: The User Login Screen (Copyright CA, Inc., Reprinted by Permission.)

After logging into the system the user is presented with the Reservation Manager where they can request virtual machines, review the status of their requests and even connect to the virtual machines after they are created (figure 18.2).

Figure 18-2: Starting the Reservation System (Copyright CA, Inc., Reprinted by Permission.)

After selecting the "reserve a system" button, the user is presented with a list of templates from which they can choose as a starting point for their virtual machine (figure 18.3).

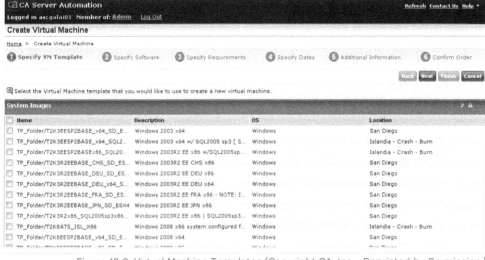

Figure 18-3: Virtual Machine Templates (Copyright CA, Inc., Reprinted by Permission.)

Next, in figure 18-4, the user selects any additional software that they want automatically installed on their virtual machines after creation. Note that different groups have access to different sets of software and additional permissions and workflows can be built automatically into the provisioning process. This is very useful depending on the software chosen. If a user wants to install Firefox, for example, that does not cost the agency any additional for licenses, but perhaps other software does incur additional charges that should be accounted for properly or perhaps passed to that department.

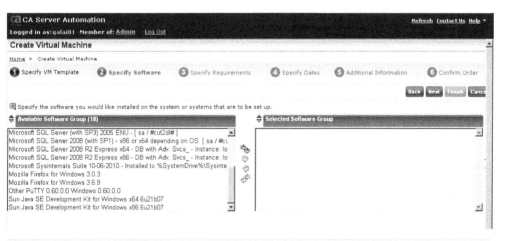

Figure 18-4: Selecting additional software packages
(Copyright CA, Inc., Reprinted by Permission.)

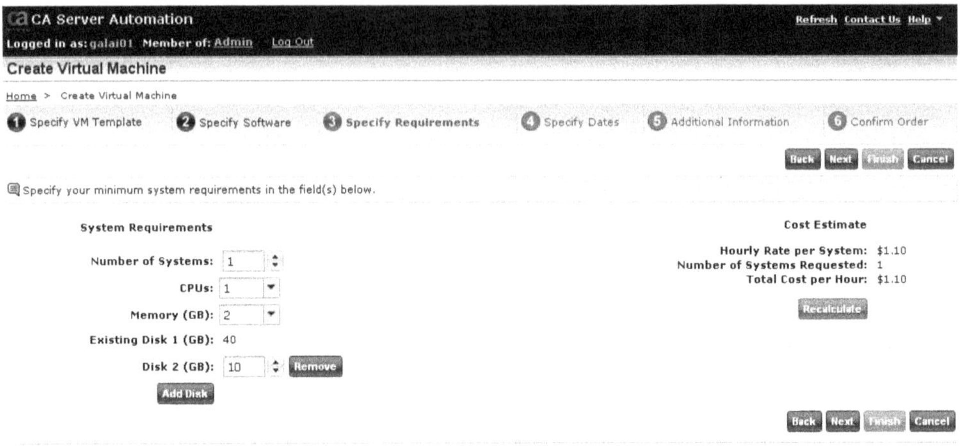

Figure 18-5: Specifying the Virtual Machine Requirements
(Copyright CA, Inc., Reprinted by Permission.)

Next the user selects the physical attributes of the system that he wants, such as number of CPUs and amount of memory, etc. (figure 18-5). Cost estimates are shown to the user at this point. As he chooses additional resources, the cost data changes automatically, based on pricing information assigned by the administrator during the system installation and configuration. There are many different ways to calculate and present the cost data to the user.

Next the user chooses how long they want the virtual machine(s) to be in use (figure 18-6). Notice that the maximum reserve is set by the administrator for each group. As well, other restrictions like number of machines, total memory usage, and many others are all

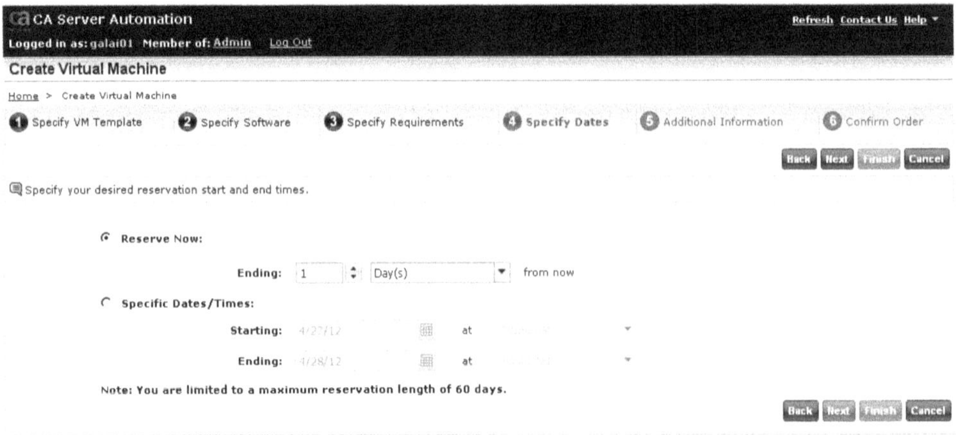

Figure 18-6: Specifying dates. (Copyright CA, Inc., Reprinted by Permission.)

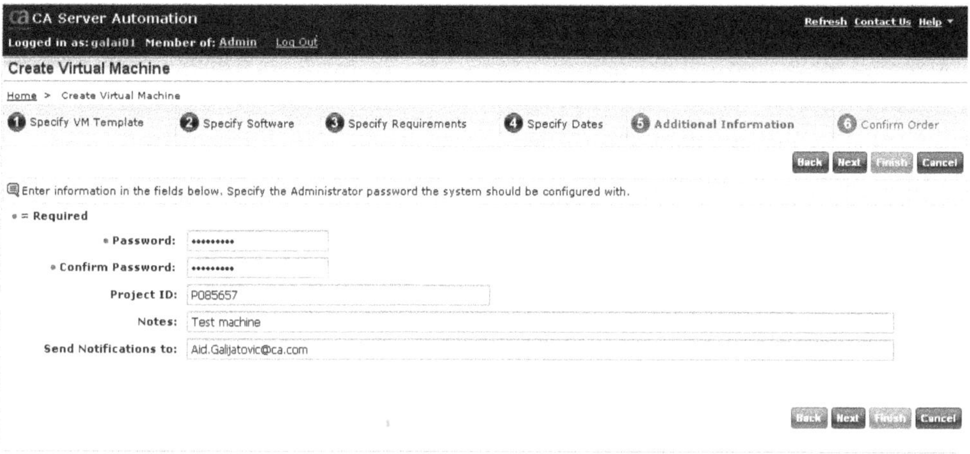

Figure 18-7: Almost finished with the request (Copyright CA, Inc., Reprinted by Permission.)

set by the administrators. We'll see a sampling of their screens in a minute.

Now the user selects the administrator password for the system as well as the email address for notifications. The user is notified when the machine(s) have been provisioned and are ready for use or each time an approval that is needed is obtained (figure 18-7).

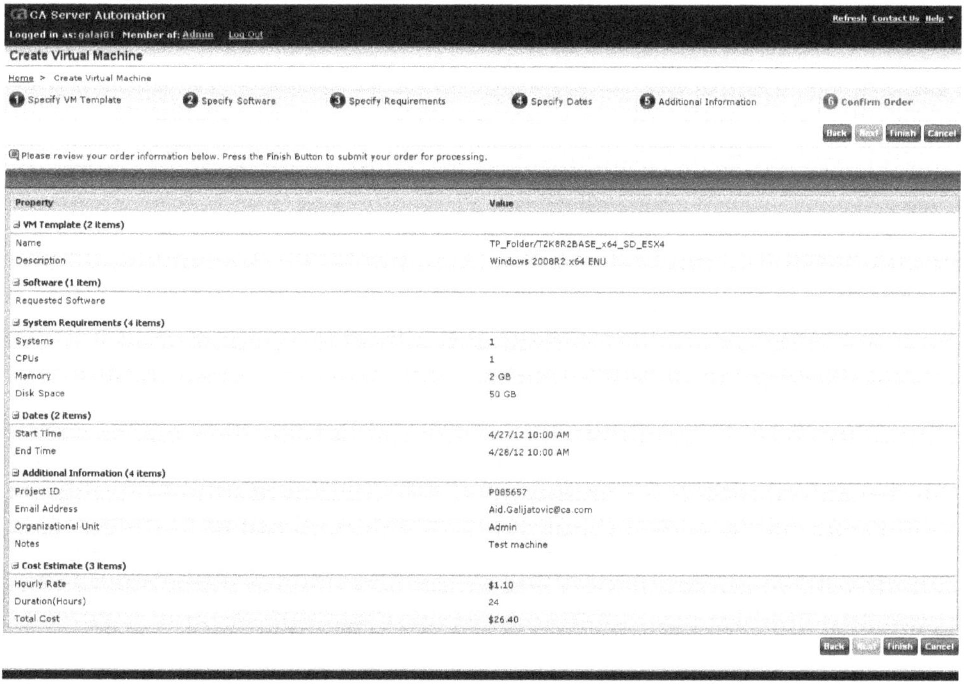

Figure 18-8: The Confirmation Screen (Copyright CA, Inc., Reprinted by Permission.)

In figure 18-8, the user is presented with a confirmation screen. This is the last chance to change options before the provisioning starts.

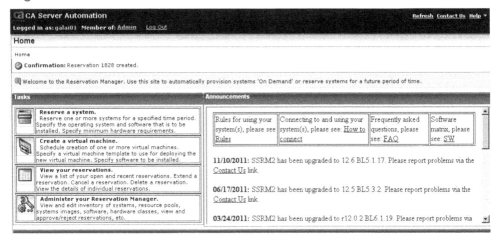

Figure 18-9: The Status Screen (Copyright CA, Inc., Reprinted by Permission.)

Now the user is presented with the status screen (figure 18-9) which shows the creation status. Again, if the user does not want to wait, alerts will be sent at every step of the creation process (figure 18-9). See the status bar under the "My Reserved Systems" banner (figure 18-2.)

CA Automation Suite for Clouds – The Administrator's View
That's it for the user side of things. Simple, right? Now let's turn to the administrator's view. The administrator creates services and establishes the rules around which they can be ordered, how many can be ordered at a time, what groups there are, what services those groups can order, and other administrative functions. As you can see in figure 18-10, the administrator's view provides a wealth of information about your services: which ones are running, how many are running, how much of your resources they are using, etc. Using a very well-done interface, administrators can quickly obtain all of the information they need to manage their infrastructure. By setting up this system, administrators manage the overall infrastructure, but the day-to-day minutiae of virtual machine adds/deletes/changes are handled within the permissions assigned automatically to your users.

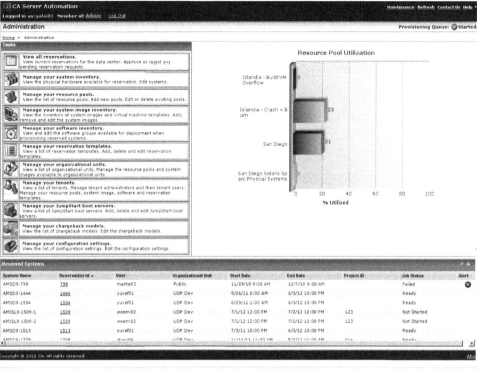

Figure 18-10: The Administrator's View (Copyright CA, Inc., Reprinted by Permission.)

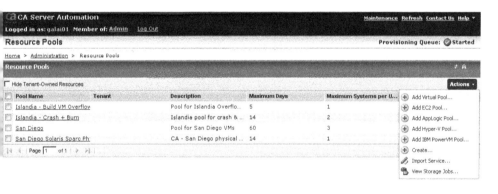

Figure 18-11: Resource Pools (Copyright CA, Inc., Reprinted by Permission.)

In figure 18-11 you can see the resource pools. The administrator can assign pools based on groups within the organization, or for different projects or many other ways. The system is very flexible to suit the many use cases across a wide variety of customers. In figure 18-12, you can see how easy it is to create a new resource pool.

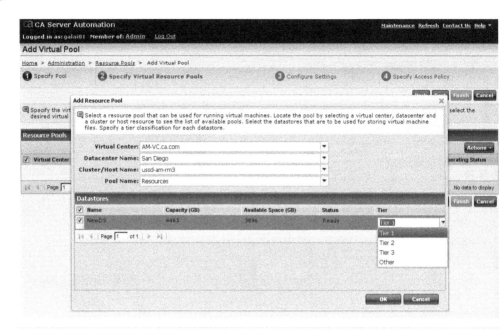

Figure 18-12. Creating a new Resource Pool. (Copyright CA, Inc., Reprinted by Permission.)

Figure 18-13 shows the system images which make up the templates from which users can request machines.

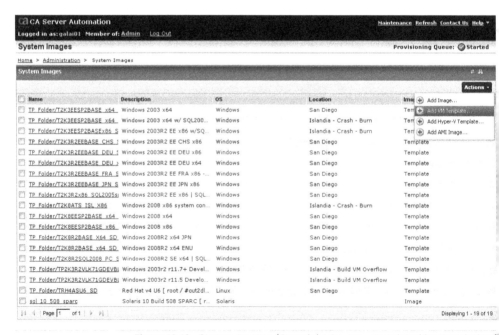

Figure 18-13: System Images (Copyright CA, Inc., Reprinted by Permission.)

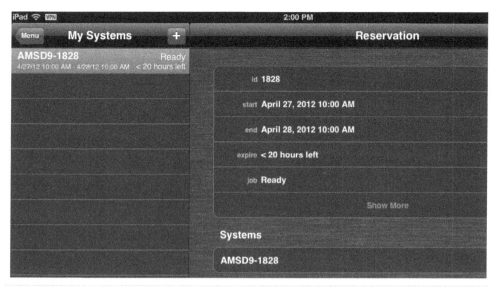

Figure 18-14: The iPad interface. (Copyright CA, Inc., Reprinted by Permission.)

There is a lot that we do not have time to show you about the CA Automation Suite, but suffice to day that I am a big fan. It's easy to use, very complete and it works well with the service creation software called AppLogic that we will get to in just a minute. But

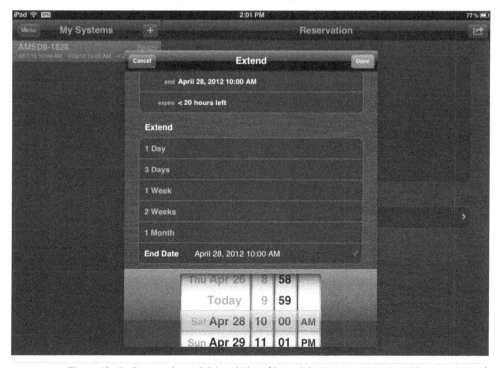

Figure 18-15: Requesting Additional Time (Copyright CA, Inc., Reprinted by Permission.)

Figure 18-16: A new reservation (Copyright CA, Inc., Reprinted by Permission.)

before we do, I have to show you one last very cool item in the CA arsenal. Ready for this? CA Systems actually has an iPad interface from which users can manage their requests and their machines. Figure 18-14 shows this software.

You can even request additional machines right from your iPad (figure 18-15). In this figure, the user is requesting an extension to their existing virtual machine.

In figure 18-16, the user is requesting a new virtual machine from their iPad.

CA AppLogic

One of the many questions I get as I meet with public sector customers around the beltway is: "How do I create services?" Because the process of creating services that IT delivers to their customers is relatively new, IT administrators need a tool to easily and quickly create, edit, and even delete services that are pushed out to the users. Here's how a Platform Architect would use AppLogic™ to create "services" on a private Cloud that users will subsequently request by logging into a portal.

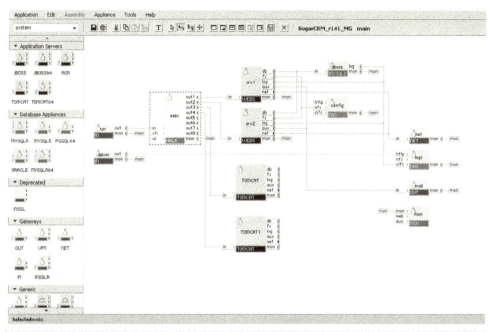

Figure 18-17: The CA AppLogic Application Editor (Copyright CA, Inc., Reprinted by Permission.)

The Application Editor, figure 18-17, is used to create single or multi-tier applications. In this example, we are creating a SugarCRM application, a very popular open source Customer Relationship Management System, which requires load-balanced web/app servers, database servers and storage and finally, interfaces to the mail sub-system and a .NET environment. The gray boxes represent external interfaces. We have set up two. One is for users to access the load-balanced (webs), web/application servers (srv1 and srv2). The other one is for the administrator to directly access the logs of the system, which reside on NAS storage (nas) and are presented to him via HTTP. In addition, the web/app servers store their config data on NAS storage (nas) and interface to the mail server (mail – external interface) and the .NET system. By adding and moving blocks (or virtual machines) around and connecting the interfaces (the lines in our figure), we have assembled a system that we can package together and present to others to request and use.

There is also shell console access to each and every virtual server or building block in the system as shown in figure 18-18.

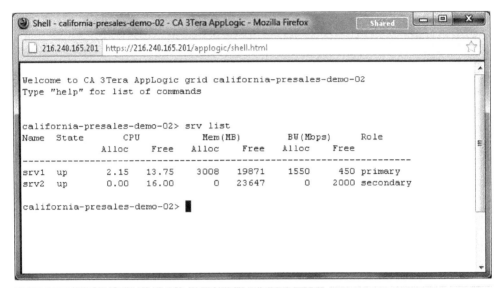

Figure 18-18: The Shell console (Copyright CA, Inc., Reprinted by Permission.)

The dashboard presents the salient performance factors for each virtual server within your environment, figure 18-19.

Figure 18-19: The AppLogic Dashboard (Copyright CA, Inc., Reprinted by Permission.)

The AppLogic system is a complete and easy-to-use system for creating software solutions that your users can order. You can use AppLogic to create the platforms, and then employ the CA Automation Suite for Clouds to deliver them to your users.

CHAPTER 19

Hybrid Case Study 1 -

Los Alamos National Labs

The Agency:
Los Alamos National Labs

Their Challenge:
Finding a more efficient way to deliver services to their users

Their Solution:
After virtualizing their servers, they incorporated a Hybrid Cloud solution

Los Alamos National Labs (LANL) is responsible for assuring the safety and reliability of the nation's nuclear deterrent. In 1943, the Laboratory was established as Site Y of the Manhattan Project for a single purpose: to design and build an atomic bomb. On July 16, 1945, the world's first atomic bomb was detonated 200 miles south of Los Alamos on the Alamogordo bombing range. The scientists at the Laboratory had successfully turned the atom into a weapon.

Today, Los Alamos National Labs has a more strategic focus on worker safety and security awareness. A variety of research programs support the Laboratory's basic mission: *maintaining the safety, security, and reliability of the nation's nuclear deterrent without the need to return to underground testing.*

But what does that have to do with Cloud? Los Alamos National Labs was one of the first government agencies to implement a Hybrid Cloud. Not only were they one of the first government agencies, they were one of the first in the country – period! And the innovator behind it is already implementing it across several Department of Energy Labs.

I recently interviewed Anil Karmel, Solutions Architect at Los Alamos and the architect of this project. He is the brains behind one of the first Hybrid Clouds in use today. In fact, he was so ahead of the curve that he actually worked with VMware to improve their vCloud product as it went through the beta testing process before general release to the public.

To review, a Hybrid Cloud is a combination of an on-premise private or community Cloud (called a Cloud cell) and a public Cloud (another cell) managed as one large Cloud implementation. One of the things I learned from Anil was that he did not start out to convert the entire agency. And he didn't set out to build a Hybrid Cloud. He started by virtualizing his then-current infrastructure using VMware. Even at this stage in the evolutionary

Gap	Alignment
Servers distributed in multiple data centers	Reduction in number of servers will enable consolidation into fewer data center facilities
Limited data center floor space, power, and cooling resources	Reduction in number of servers will reduce data center requirements
Need to retire unsupported platforms	Unsupported platforms can be replaced by virtual servers
Slow server provisioning cycle-time	New environments provisioned without purchasing and installing additional physical servers
Limited hardware for disaster recovery	Environments can be restored onto different hardware. Hardware replaced by new virtual servers and servers retired during future refresh cycles can be utilized for DR site.

Figure 19-1: Virtualization Challenges at LANL (from VMware)

process, there were some good reasons to move to a Hybrid Cloud (figure 19-1).

His first VMware cluster, assembled in 2006, consisted of thirteen HP ProLiant DL585 servers, each with 4 dual-core AMD Opteron processors, 32 GB of memory and redundant network and fiber channel cards. For storage, he used 250 TB of total storage shared across several HP EVA SAN devices. That first cluster also included:

- A total of 400 virtual machines running in a 13 Server VMware DRS/HA cluster
- Average resource utilization of 85%
- 30:1 consolidation ratio

Anil saw the tremendous cost savings in power, cooling and space that were possible by virtualizing an infrastructure. He de-commissioned 105 physical servers and shut down 3 data centers just by virtualizing his existing infrastructure. Last, but certainly not least, Anil realized amazing electrical power savings from decommissioning physical servers and datacenters. The actual savings are shown in figure 19-2.

The initial projection called for a return on investment (ROI) of two years, but the actual ROI he achieved was only nine months from the inception of the project!

Servers (kWh/yr)	400 Physical Servers	13 Physical Hosts	Energy Savings
Direct	1,392,214	56,822	1,335,392
Indirect	510,800	20,847	489,953
Total	1,903,014	77,669	**1,825,345**

Figure 19-2: Electrical Savings at LANL from Virtualization

But why start with virtualization? In Anil's opinion, "Leapfrogging virtualization to go to Cloud only means that you are setting yourself up for failure. Virtualize, then build best practices, understand what that means, then build the Cloud on top of that."

When he completed the virtualization project he then moved on to create the Hybrid Cloud environment, using his Private Cloud and the vCloud implementation of the public Cloud provider, Terremark. But what was Anil's motivation? Hadn't he already accomplished a lot with his virtualization cluster? He certainly had! But there were other requirements that came to light:

- Anil wanted a self-service web portal to automatically request and provision virtual servers
- He wanted the green IT savings dynamically computed and displayed on the website
- He wanted his cluster to include LifeCycle Management and Chargeback
- He wanted to support a variety of operating systems, including
  - Microsoft Windows
  - Red Hat Enterprise Linux
  - Sun Solaris

He also knew that in order to attract customers to his self-service environment, he would need to offer certain value-added services that were not automatically offered in a standard virtualized environment, including:

- Full backup/recovery of virtual machines
- vCenter Management consoled administrators to support the underlying infrastructure
- No ongoing infrastructure refresh costs
- New virtual servers automatically provisioned for the customer

In practice, this meant that once the virtual machines were requested and provisioned from the self-service portal, all the user had to worry about was the security plan for the virtual machine and the system administration and maintenance of the operating system and the applications. The whole point was to use the principle of "Attraction" versus "Authoritarianism." They practiced this principle in the design. Anil said that although they were not fully virtualized, they had designed a system "for the 80%." In other words, while this system didn't cover everyone's needs at LANL, it met the needs of 80% of the users. For them, that was a huge success. Anil told me that there still are many physical servers left at Los Alamos. Many of those users elected to stay on them for one reason or another. Maybe they felt the difficulty of migrating their workload to a virtual environment outweighed the benefits. Or maybe they decided to stay on that physical machine until it was time for a refresh cycle. Anil decided that trying to design a system for 100% of the needs of the engineers at LANL was impossible. Rather than give up, he decided to design a system that was good for 80% of their needs. As you can tell from his savings numbers, even a system designed for 80% of the users can have a huge financial impact on an agency's budget.

Before moving to the Hybrid Cloud model, LANL decided it was time for a tech refresh. This time, the customer elected to go with a blade architecture that consisted of the following components:
- HP ProLiant c7000 Blade Infrastructure
    - HP Virtual Connect Fiber Channel / Flex-10 Ethernet with six 10GB Network Feeds per Chassis
    - HP ProLiant BL490c Virtualization Blade
        - Two Six-Core Intel Xeon processors

- 144GB RAM
  - Internal SSD drives to host the VMware ESXi Boot Image
- NetApp V-Series and 2PB of Tier 2 (SATA) Storage
  - Providing management and virtualization of existing storage arrays
  - New data de-duplication capabilities previously not present
  - Snapshots of virtual machines for backup and restore

When the hardware refresh was done, it was on to the Cloud! They developed a web portal which, among other things, displays information regarding the service and a form to request a system. It also displays a Green IT calculation, which delineates how many kilowatt-hours LANL has saved by using the Hybrid Cloud. A screen shot of the portal is shown in figure 19-3. They also implemented two additional products from VMware: the vCloud Director, which enables the private Cloud and provides a web-based interface for users to consume Cloud resources, and the vShield virtual appliance which is used to implement, manage, and maintain the appropriate security policies in the private or Hybrid Cloud. Finally,

Figure 19-3: The Los Alamos National Labs Self Service Portal

LANL implemented Microsoft SharePoint and used that as the workflow engine, including the lifecycle management functionality and the integration point for the internal systems like Chargeback and Hostmaster Domain Registration System.

On the user side, there is one place, and only one place, to go to create a new virtual machine: the web portal. There are no forms, therefore no confusion. Figure 19-4 shows another screenshot with the one button that is necessary for the user to get started. During this process, the user elects to either put their virtual machines in the Cloud node, which is located within the LANL firewalls, or out in the Terremark Cloud.

Figure 19-4: The "Create Server" button on the LANL portal

In figure 19-5, we see the options the user has for creating this specific windows virtual machine. As the user/requester moves the sliders, they are given immediate feedback about how much they will be charged each month for their virtual machine. Cost is not the only issue at hand at LANL. Time savings are critical, too. Anil explained, "Average provisioning time for a physical servers was 30 days. Now when using the Cloud it is 30 minutes. That's

≣inside

Computing   Employees   Environment   Finance   News   Safety   Science   Security   Services

INFRASTRUCTURE ON DEMAND

SUPPORT

Please refer to the FAQ page for all general questions.

For further info, contact

Tier 3 On-Call Support (after hours only).

Requester

J Number

Name

Anil Karmel

Responsible Line Manager (System Owner)

Clear

Figure 19-5: Selecting and Sizing a Windows VM

the agility and flexibility we were looking to provide our users and provide it securely."

One significant advantage offered by this portal is that it shows the users how much they are saving right on the portal (figure 19-6). It

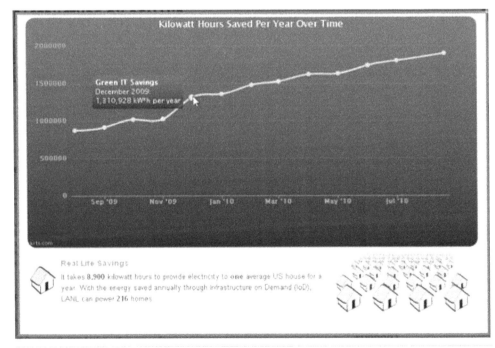

Figure 19-6: The real savings as displayed on the LANL portal

also puts that savings into real world terms for the average user who may not be thinking about the green aspects of virtualization and Cloud computing.

I really like the option for yellow, or on-premise compute

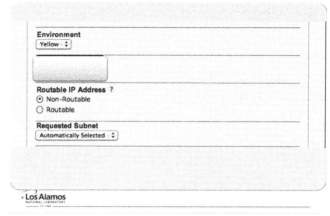

Figure 19-7: Selecting "Yellow" for on Premise

resources, as in figure 19-7.

The user can request a more "Green" alternative, meaning that the virtual machine will reside in the Terremark Cloud cell as in figure 19-8.

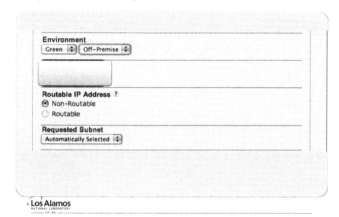

Figure 19-8: Going "Green"

Figure 19-9 shows that users even have 3 different levels of service from which to choose for their virtual machine.

Figure 19-10 shows the management console that is displayed to the user with private

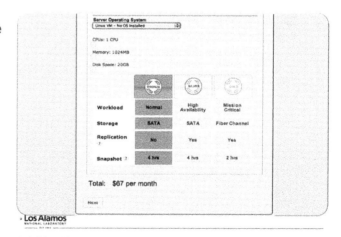

Figure 19-9: Multiple Service Levels

information blocked out. As you can see, the vDC is either LANL or Terremark. All of the workloads or virtual machines for this user happen to reside within the LANL firewall.

Anil has won several awards for his work. He was the recipient of:
- The 2009 NNSA "Best in Class Pollution Prevention Award" for Server Virtualization
- The *Information Week* 500 Award as top Government IT Innovator in 2011
- The National CyberSecurity Innovator Award, October, 2011

When I asked Anil about the success of the project, he told me it was critical to engage and win support from key stakeholders before embarking on a major consolidation or Cloud computing initiative. Anil and his team focused hard on auditing their legacy environment and mapping the chargeback relationships between

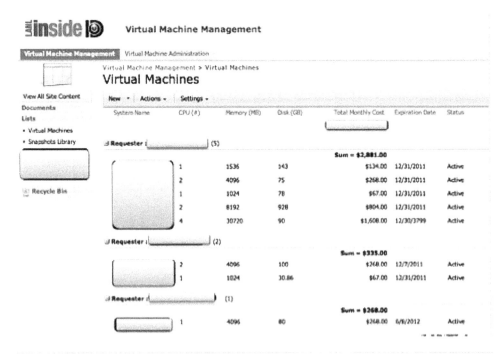

Figure 19-10: Infrastructure on Demand Management Console

computing resources and the business customers who pay the bill. He firmly believes that in order to really change things, you need to show your customers how they can get better service at less cost and – more importantly – how that applies not just at the installation level, but to their program and budget, as well.

Anil speaks on Cloud now and again. If you are considering Cloud for your agency and get an opportunity to be in the audience, make it a point to be there! If you follow in his footsteps, you will be following a true innovator!

Today, Anil is forging ahead with Cloud and is looking to the future. He believes that the future of Cloud is really "Your Cloud," giving everyone autonomy while provisioning through a common Cloud framework. What is his advice for those looking to implement their own Cloud? "The Cloud is not a panacea. There are real use cases and there is real ROI data. Understand virtualization and what Cloud is and apply that capability to your specific requirements. Then select vendor products that meet them."

20

Other Uses for the Cloud – Mechanical Turk

A new and really innovative use of the Cloud is called crowdsourcing. People? Yes. People. Amazon Web Services has a new use for their Cloud called Mechanical Turk™. Here is an example. Suppose you have a million digital images and you need to determine how many of those images have a red ball in them. This is a very repetitive task that is difficult for a computer to perform automatically. But it's perfect for Mechanical Turk.

In Mechanical Turk, agencies place work to be done in an AWS catalog, then workers (housewives, college students, etc) decide if they want to perform these tasks, based on the requirements and the pay. For each transaction that is completed – in our example a picture is examined and put into a "no red ball" or "red ball" pile – the worker is paid the accepted transaction rate for that job. A complete billing and payment system is built into the AWS Cloud offering; there is even a worker reputation system included with it. Going back to our example, if a given worker (number 432567092, let's say) puts 4 out of 100 images that have red balls into the "no red ball" pile, that indicates that worker isn't all that reliable. In that case, the organization needing the work decides that the worker in question is not permitted to work on their tasks. Or maybe they decide that they need to create a double check and verification system by having three workers look at each of the image and have at least 2 out of the three correctly classify them.

Using Cloud technology to have workers bid on repetitive tasks to get them done quickly and reliably is a pretty novel use of the Cloud. In fact, the U.S. military is already using this technology to identify images. Mechanical Turk is best used for high-volume, low-level tasks that require human intervention. Here are some examples:

- Business processes that require human intervention
- Moderation, including adding comments or met-data to video or photos
- Entity extraction
- Categorization
- Data cleansing

Some examples of the HITs (Human Intelligence Tasks) that are currently available for users to sign up and work are:
- Select the correct spelling for these search terms
- Is this website suitable for a general audience?
- Find the item number for the product in this image
- Rate the search results for these keywords

- Are these two products the same?
- Choose the appropriate category for products
- Categorize the tone of this article
- Translate a paragraph from English to French

Signing up as a worker is very simple. Candidates register at **https://www.mturk.com/mturk/welcome?variant=worker.**

Mechanical Turk allows you to:
- **Define your HITs**, including the specific output desired, the format of the output, how you display your work items and how much you will pay to have them completed.
- **Load HITs into the marketplace** to be completed (you can load millions).
- **Qualify your workforce** (if you desire); if special skills are required to complete your tasks, you can require that workers who work on your HITs pass a qualification. Or you can require that a worker complete a certain percentage of their tasks correctly, or that they have completed a minimum number of previous HITs.
- **Only pay for quality work.** You have the ability to review the results and accept or reject them. You only pay for accepted work.
- **Retrieve the results.** Using the provided web services APIs, developers can retrieve the results and integrate them directly into their applications.

Of course, AWS does not provide this service for free. They take a small percentage, currently 10%, of the fees paid to workers on a given project or HIT. The minimum is currently set to $0.005 per HIT.

Every day new uses for the Cloud emerge. But this may truly be one of the most unique.

CHAPTER 21

Other Uses Case Study 1 -

John Hopkins University

The Agency:
Johns Hopkins University, Department of Computer Science

Their Challenge:
Creating standardized translations of multiple Arabic dialects

Their Solution:
Employing AWS Mechanical Turk to crowdsource Arabic dialects

Language translation is fairly standardized these days for most of the Romance or Germanic languages. Even the free web-based translators will do an adequate job of translating English a number of languages and vice versa.

But what happens with Arabic, a language that is spoken by over 250 million people with many dialects? While the translation for what is commonly called MSA (Modern Standard Arabic) to English is usually very good, MSA is rarely spoken throughout the region.[32] Instead the spoken and written versions of the language have many regional dialects which differ widely from MSA and from each other. When machine translation is applied to any one of the dialects, the translation to English is almost always unsatisfactory in terms of both correctness and readability.

So what is the answer? In natural language processing research, translations are most often made using in statistical machine translation (SMT), where systems are trained using sentence-aligned documents in two languages. SMT owes its existence to data like Canadian laws which must be published in both French and English. SMT can be applied to any language pair for which there is sufficient data. It has been shown to produce state-of-the-art results for language pairs like MSA Arabic–English, where there is ample data,[33] but not so with various dialects.

I encountered a similar problem the first time I went to Puerto Rico. I had studied Spanish I, II, III and IV, so I felt I was ready to go and really enjoy myself. If you have studied Spanish, you already know that you are taught Castilian (or textbook Spanish). It may be spoken in some parts of Spain, but most of the other Spanish-speaking regions have different dialects. A person speaking one dialect may make little or no sense to a person speaking another. I distinctly remember trying to stumble out, "Let's get a car," or something to that effect, using the phrase "el coche" for car. My Puerto Rican friend laughed and blurted out, "Oh, you mean, el carro," which was their dialectic word for car. They had no understanding of Castilian Spanish – and I had just had my first lesson in dialects!

I related this story to Professor Chris Callison-Burch, Department of Computer Science, Johns Hopkins University. He told me that my story was even more common in the Middle East.

With tensions in that area of the world erupting often, accurately translating Arabic dialects is extremely important to the US Government and many others.

But what was the best, and most cost-effective, way to obtain accurate dialectic Arabic translations? That was the problem facing two professors of computer science at Johns Hopkins University.

One option was to simply hire translators to create parallel data. That option quickly becomes prohibitively expensive – by some estimates half a million dollars – just to translate enough word pairs to teach the machine language translator enough to translate one dialect.

Another option was to employ AWS Mechanical Turk. If you're wondering what this has to do with Cloud...and how a language translation task could possibly apply to case studies drawn from the public sector, read on.

First, this translation project was supported by the Human Language Technology Center of Excellence, by the DARPA GALE program under Contract No. HR0011-06-2-0001, and by Raytheon BBN Technologies.

Second, after learning about Amazon's Mechanical Turk, the professors decided that this might be an excellent way to try to translate the millions of words they had in each dialect, then feed this data into their machine language translation system. They needed to locate a pool of native speakers for each dialect to translate the millions of words and do it quickly, inexpensively and reliably. Using the web to locate native speakers appeared to be the most viable tool for the researchers, since these resources were not available locally in Baltimore, Maryland, where Johns Hopkins is located.

Professors Omar F. Zaidan and Chris Callison-Burch published a white paper where they proved that they could create low cost translations via crowdsourcing.[34] Using the Mechanical Turk features of Amazon Web Services, they quantitatively and objectively compared an existing dataset of professionally-prepared translations for the Urdu language with the same translations prepared by non-professionals. While hiring a professional translator ensures a certain degree of accuracy, using non-professionals carries a significant risk of poor quality translation. They showed it was possible to get high quality translations, even though the translators were non-professionals, by soliciting multiple translations, redundantly editing them, then selecting the best of the bunch.

An example of the type of problem they faced was an Urdu headline which was professionally translated as "Barack Obama: America Will Adopt a New Iran Strategy." When translated by a non-professional, the same headline came back as, "Barak Obam will do a new policy with Iran" and from another as "Barak Obama and America weave new evil strategies against Iran."

To select the best translations they used a machine-learning-inspired approach that assigned a score to each translation that they collected. These scores were based on such discriminators as country of residence, edit rate from other translations, number of years speaking English, etc.

---

34 Crowdsourcing Translation: Professional Quality from Non-Professionals, Omar F. Zaidan and Chris Callison-Burch, Department of Computer Science, John Hopkins University, Baltimore, MD 21218, USA

They learned a lot about translations and about using Mechanical Turk. As a matter of fact, Professor Callison-Burch said that at first he thought that Mechanical Turk would not work for their purposes and that he "actually spent $20.00 of my own money to try it out." Now he says, "I love being proved wrong when I think that you can't do something on Mechnical Turk and it turns out that you can."

Success with Mechanical Turk has a lot to do with how you ask the questions. For example, the professors learned early on to post the questions to be translated into short sentences – not long pages – to improve accuracy. They also learned to display the sentences to be translated as pictures so that the "Turkers" (AWS term for the people that actually perform the crowd-sourced work) would not copy and paste the sentence into a machine language translator, then simply copy and paste the answer into the response box.

After they designed the HIT (Human Intelligence Task) and so-licited responses, the professors did post-edited versions of the translations as well as ranking judgments of the HITs. They paid the Turkers $.10 to translate a sentence, $.25 to edit a set of 10 sentences, and $.06 to rank a set of four translation groups. For a total of 10 post-edited translations, the total cost was:

Translation Costs: $716.80

Editing Costs: $447.50

Ranking Costs: $134.40

The in-depth details of the math behind their analysis can be found in their whitepaper. Suffice it to say, the professors con-cluded that it is possible to obtain high-quality translations from non-professional translators, and that the cost is an order of magnitude cheaper than using professionals. They also noted that crowdsourcing (and Mechanical Turk, in particular) provided access to languages that currently fall outside of the scope of statistical machine translation research.

Their results spurred them on to bigger and even more significant discoveries. Knowing that it was now possible to get what they wanted, they decided to translate some of the various Arabic dialects that are prevalent in the Middle East.

Their first problem was finding enough words to translate. Spoken varieties of the Arabic language differ widely among themselves, depending on things such as the geographic distribution of the speakers, as well as the socio-economic levels of the speakers. There are also issues surrounding phonology, morphology, lexicon and even syntax that make some varieties of these dialects mutually incomprehensible.[35] In order to teach the machine language translator, the professors needed to amass a large number of words in each dialect.

After discarding many other sources , the Arabic Online Commentary dataset they created was based on reader commentary from the online versions of three Arabic newspapers: Al-Ghad from Jordan, Al-Riyadh from Saudi Arabia, and Al-Youm Al-Sabe' from Egypt. The common dialects in those countries are Levantine, Gulf, and Egyptian, respectively.

They crawled through webpages corresponding to articles published during a 6-month period, from early April 2010 to early October 2010. This resulted in crawling about 150K urls, 86.1K of which included reader commentary. The data consists of 1.4M comments, corresponding to 52.1M words.

They also extracted the following information for each comment when available:
- The url of the relevant newspaper article
- The date and time of the comment

35 The Arabic Online Commentary Dataset: an Annotated Dataset of Informal Arabic with High Dialectal Content, Omar F. Zaidan and Chris Callison-Burch, Department of Computer Science, John Hopkins University, Blatimore, MD, 21218, USA.

- The author ID associated with the comment
- The subtitle header
- The author's e-mail address
- The author's geographical location

Using this data source offered several advantages:
- A large amount of data was available, with more data available on a daily basis
- The data was publicly accessible
- The data existed in a structured, consistent format, and was easy to extract
- The data contained a high level of topic relevance

Once they had the words, they turned again to Mechanical Turk. The professors selected a small subset (142,530 of the 3.1M available sentences) for translation. They kept the instructions very simple, aug-menting them with the map shown in figure 21-1, with the Arabic names of the dialects.

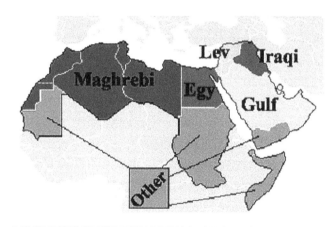

The sentences were grouped into 14,253 sets of 10 sentences each. For each group of sentences, the Turkers identified

Figure 21-1: A map of the various Arabic dialects

the level of dialectical Arabic and which dialect it was (if any). Each Turker was paid $.05 per screen; each screen was com-pleted by three distinct workers. This is an important aspect of Mechanical Turk. You have complete control over how many work-ers you want to look at and act upon your work, how many have to agree for the answer to be "correct," and even what grade of workers are allowed to work on your HITs. In this particular case, the professors considered a sentence to be dialectical it was labeled as such by at least two workers. Conversely, two workers identifying a sentence as MSA Arabic completed its identification.

Now they had the sentences and they had them by dialect. They turned again to Mechanical Turk to translate the Levantine and Egyptian sentences into English. They then asked a series of native Arabic speakers to score a sample of each worker's translations. These high scoring workers were promoted to a "preferred worker" pool and they were paid a higher rate for their work. Unlike their initial Urdu test, where there were only enough words to prove the hypothesis that Mechanical Turk could be successfully used for this type of task, but not enough words to teach a machine language translator, they were now able to translate 1.1 million words of Levantine and 380,000 words of Egyptian. The total cost per word, including the judges, worked out to 2.9 cents per word. They managed to produce a Dialect-English reference document containing 1.5 million words for a grand total of about $40K!

Based upon the success of this research, Professor Callison-Burch has gone on to study 7 Indian dialects and, using Mechanical Turk, has translated 500,000 words in a 5-day period. This could have a major impact during a period of natural disasters when translations of obscure languages need to be able to be done quickly in order to assist the rescuers and aid workers.

According to Callison-Burch, "The real issue is not cost but speed. We can cut these tasks into small chunks. This is similar to a project like SETI@home (a scientific experiment that uses Internet-connected computers in the Search for Extraterrestrial Intelligence) but with human computational cycles."

When asked about possible drawbacks, he continued, "there really aren't any with the Mechanical Turk Program itself. It's all about designing the task in a way so you can validate it. Insert

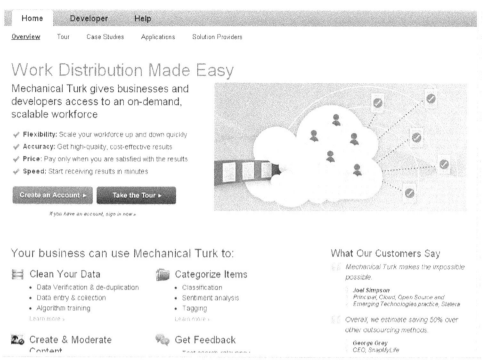

Figure 21-2: Mechanical Turk home Screen

Gold Standard questions for which you have the answers. This helps a lot. And also, design the task in a way which is under-standable for non-experts. That's really key."

Getting started with Mechanical Turk is very simple. Because it takes no time at all to get up and running, I am only going to include a few screen shots. First, just point your browser to **https://requester. mturk.com/** and request an account (as shown in figure 21-2).

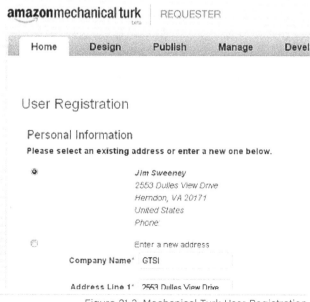

Figure 21-3: Mechanical Turk User Registration

Figure 21-4: The Requester Page

Then simply sign up using the links as in figure 21-3.

You are now ready to begin.

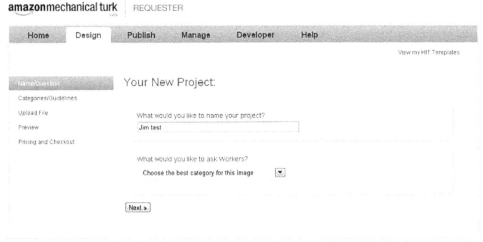

Figure 21-5: Naming your project

A "requester" is the person requesting the work. Start design-ing your task by indicating what kind of work you are asking the "Turkers" to perform (figure 21-4).

Next, name your project, figure 21-5.

Continue with the wizard by filling in the classification questions as I have done in figure 21-6.

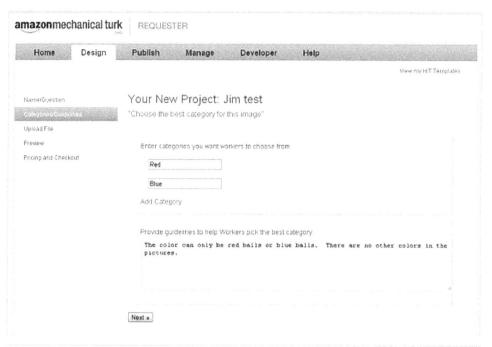

Figure 21-6: Project Category

I have selected a rather simple task: asking workers to identify a red ball or a blue ball in each of the pictures they are shown. Upload your items (pictures, in my case) and your project is ready to begin. Obviously there is a lot more customization possible, but this shows you how easy it is to get started with Mechanical Turk!

Cloud is not just used in the IT world, but in the research world as well. This is a unique example of the power of the Public Cloud by inexpensively sourcing users with different skill sets half way around the globe to perform repetitive, but human necessary, tasks. I hope this example will start you thinking of other potential new and innovative uses for the Public Cloud. As this case study shows, Amazon has really come up with unique application of Cloud with Mechanical Turk.

CHAPTER
22

Summary

Were you one of the ones who asked, "What's the buzz about Cloud and why should I care?" By now, I hope you understand what Cloud is (and what it isn't), how the various service models and deployment models intersect, and through our real-world case studies, how you might be able to take advantage of Cloud in your organization or agency.

First let's review the various Cloud Deployment Models:

Public Cloud – Run by companies or individuals, they are outside of your firewall, and are open to use by the general "public."

Private Cloud – The opposite of Public Clouds; these Clouds are built by you or for you, reside inside your firewalls, and are solely for use by your organization.

Community Cloud – Private or Public Clouds set up solely for users with a common interest (or community) to use.

Hybrid Clouds – A mixture (or hybrid) of Public and Private Clouds; uses the infrastructure that you have in place, but lets you tap into a Public Cloud for its massive scalability, access from multiple locations, and other advantages.

Now let's review the Cloud Service Models:

IaaS or Infrastructure as a Service provides additional infrastructure (servers or storage) when you need it, only paying for it when you use it, and then releasing it to be used by someone else for another purpose. Amazon Web Services, or AWS and Terremark are both great examples of public IaaS Cloud providers.

SaaS or Software as a Service permits you to use software for as long as you need it, paying only what you use. The most popular example of a public SaaS Cloud is Salesforce.com. There are many SaaS providers – some of the most well-known are Microsoft, HyperOffice, Sonian, and Google Apps.

PaaS or Platform as a Service offers you the ability to rapidly develop and deploy web applications. The two most commonly-used of these are public offerings: Windows Azure and Google App Engine.

All Service Models can be deployed within each of the Deployment models, which adds to the confusion about Cloud.

Examples of Cloud

AWS is a good example of an IaaS Public Cloud. Conversely, the GTSI lab is a good example of a Private IaaS Cloud (really a Cloud cell). And Anil Karmel's Cloud configuration at LANL is a good example of a Hybrid IaaS Cloud.

SaaS Cloud offerings are normally Public Clouds. Microsoft and their Office 365 offering, Google and their Google Apps are both good examples. A company called Sonian offers a private SaaS Cloud. A new breed of company, they provide email archiving and e-discovery software. While this Cloud is usually deployed as a Public SaaS offering, the vendors have installed it internally on top of their existing private IaaS Cloud for security reasons. Since they meet all of the other characteristics (pay only for what you use, etc.) we can consider them a private SaaS offering.

When we consider PaaS Cloud, the most obvious examples are public, like Windows Azure and Google App Engine. Because of their private nature I'm not aware of any private PaaS offerings. There may be some, but with the tools and infrastructure you need to rapidly develop, test, and deploy web applications, it really makes the most sense in a public model.

Case Studies – Real World Examples Of Cloud Technology

Federal, state and local governments are currently using Cloud in innovative ways: from simple IaaS Clouds that take advantage of the auto-scaling features of the public providers...to Hybrid Clouds that are saving taxpayers literally millions in power and cooling while providing a more agile, flexible environment for its users...to others that have totally switched their users to SaaS applications from Microsoft and Google...to an example of Crowd Sourcing (AWS calls this Mechanical Turk) using the Cloud to source people to translate Arabic dialects!

There are many agencies within the public sector that are already using Cloud. Their requirements may vary greatly, but all have found that Cloud is a good IT tool for addressing the needs of their particular service or application.

Is Cloud Right For You?

Is there room for Cloud in your agency? Not for every service or application, but for some of them?

In the new model of IT, Cloud is just one of the many tools in your toolbox. Ideally, IT works with business or agency department heads to understand the requirements for a new service. (I am using service in the ITIL definition of the word.) Once the needs are clearly defined and agreed to, IT is tasked with sourcing that service with the agreed-to SLAs and within the agreed-to costs. Perhaps there is further discussion with the agency leadership to determine what they are willing to pay for the service. For example, IT says, "In order to keep track of your constituents, I can give you a spreadsheet for $399.00, an open source CRM tool that we host here with its associated costs, a program like Sage ACT which resides between the spreadsheet and a full blown CRM system or I can give you a SaaS-based CRM tool with all of the bells and whistles that come with it that will cost $12.00 per month per user." The job of IT is to now provide that service and manage the vendors and the associated SLAs of the service, regardless of the choice that is made.

On July 8, 2011, President Obama announced an across-the-board reduction of managed services within the government for fiscal year 2012. This announcement is encouraging many agencies to look at Cloud as an alternative to the traditional hosted models of the IT department of the past. The famous "Cloud First" policy of the former CIO, Vivek Kundra, is pushing agencies to adopt Cloud as a "go-to" strategy to get more done with less!

Getting Started With Cloud

How do you get started with Cloud? There are several things you can do.

1. There is a great workshop from HP (which we at GTSI sell and deliver in conjunction with HP) called the **Cloud Discovery Workshop**. It gets your agency executives in a room for two days to discuss Cloud, all of your challenges and all of the procedures and policies that would need to be amended in order to take advantage of Cloud. (Yes, I realize that was a shameless plug for GTSI, but you didn't expect to get through

the entire book without at least one plug for my employer, did you?)

2. There are several assessments that will help you decide which applications might be right to move to a Cloud environment. GTSI's methodology is a 7-step process, as follows:

   a. Understand the cost of running the application as is today compared to running it in the Cloud (public or private).

   b. Understand the performance of that application today.

   c. Understand which policies, procedure and governance changes will be required when and if this application is moved to the Cloud.

   d. Make a decision to migrate or not. If yes, migrate.

   e. Implement policy, procedure, and governance changes as agreed to in c).

   f. Measure the performance of the application to ensure it is greater than or equal to the previous measurement.

   g. Prove the cost difference as promised in a).

There are other assessments you could use, but frankly, if they don't tell you the cost of running the application as it is today, they are totally worthless. Although Cloud is not all about cost savings, if you do have cost savings, then you can justify the price of the migration. Without realizing cost savings, you can't. So, I repeat: if the assessment doesn't tell you the cost difference, it is probably not much good to you. The same goes for performance. If your assessment doesn't measure performance so that you can *guarantee* that the performance is the same or greater after migration, it is pretty worthless. After all, why would you move to Cloud for a downgrade in performance?

But even before you get to an assessment, how can you get started? First, you need to have an idea of what applications you might want to migrate. The following decision tree may offer some direction.

1. **Does this application process classified data?** Yes? OK. Stop. Cloud can accommodate FISMA moderate applications, but it is probably not a great place to start. Can you do it? Sure. But just like we started virtualizing web servers and file servers and print servers and not Microsoft Exchange servers, I suggest this is not the best place for you to start your Cloud experience. If you answered "no", proceed to question 2.

2. **Does this application process secure/sensitive data?** Yes? OK. Proceed with caution. Cloud can accommodate FISMA moderate applications, but just like in question 1, above, it is probably not a great place to get started with Cloud. If you answered "no," proceed to question 3.

3. **Is this a new customer application?** With a new application, you have more choices because you don't have to deal with legacy operating systems which may not be supported in a Cloud, or legacy architectures that would need too much redesign to fit into a Cloud model. Consider migrating to an IaaS Cloud. Newer applications that are at least running on x86 hardware and operating systems have a good chance of being able to be migrated to the Cloud with some simple redesign to take advantage of the flexibility, agility, availability and scalability of public IaaS Cloud. If it is an older application, and is ready to be chucked and rewritten, then treat it as a new application.

4. **Is it a desktop application?** (Like a word processor, or email) If you are near the end of your current maintenance cycle or before a major upgrade in versions, it might make sense to look at one of the many SaaS providers. For office type applications and email, there many from which to choose. We've talked about a few of them: Microsoft, Google, HyperOffice, and Sonian.

5. **Is it an enterprise application like CRM or ERP?** There are many, many SaaS offerings out there that you should evaluate. We talked about a couple of the major ones, Salesforce. com in particular. Again, the time to start looking at these is before you are up for renewal or a major upgrade.

6. **Finally, is this a new application that just needs some web servers and maybe a database?** Maybe a quick PaaS application is right for you. After all, most web applications are really serving up public data anyway. So maybe Microsoft Windows Azure or Google App Engine is the way to go here. As I write this I have heard rumors that HP will come out with their Cloud offering shortly to rival some of the major players and it will include IaaS, SaaS and PaaS offerings.

As for Private or Hybrid IaaS Clouds, there are many civilian agencies that are attempting to provide Cloud services to their fellow public sector brethren. But seriously, how can you compete with the major Cloud providers that have already built what you are now trying to build, especially as they are rapidly coming up to speed with the certifications to run your applications in their public infrastructure? Personally, I believe you would be better served by understanding your options and migrating/developing those applications that can take advantage of the public Cloud, rather than trying to compete with the public Cloud providers. They are way ahead of you in terms of infrastructure and experience for you to be successful long term.

To give you an example of what I am talking about, understand that Cloud is forcing IT to adopt a new modus operandi. IT must now work with the business/agency departments to understand their requirements, and then source the delivery of that service in the best way possible. Cloud has become another way of delivering a service to meet a set of business requirements. It is one of many options that IT must evaluate, based on the requirements of the business or organizational unit, the promised SLAs of the service, and the costs of that service.

This is how it is supposed to work. A business or organizational unit desires a service. After meeting with the business unit managers, IT agrees to a set of requirements for the service. IT then evaluates how to best deliver that service. Cloud (or rather one of the many types of Cloud) may be one option to consider.

Let's look at an example from my experience at GTSI. We will use Email as our example. If we follow the decision trail, we know:
- We are not processing classified data
- It is used by a lot of people in various locations around the US
- There will be more than 500 people using the application

At the 5,000 foot view, one could say that it might be better for us to look at a SaaS alternative to hosting our own email. That's when you really need to look at the requirements and understand what your users want, and what they are willing to pay for. In our particular case, we are very Outlook calendar centric.

You may remember the old M*A*S*H episode where Hawkeye and Trapper order takeout from Adam's Rib's near the Dearborn St. Station in Chicago? They go to the supply sergeant who will not release the "package." Their conversation went as follows:

Sergeant: There's no S47 stroke 19J accompanying.

Hawkeye (*to Trapper*): I told you we should've gotten an S47 stroke 19J accompanying! But you wouldn't listen.

Trapper (*to the sergeant*): That's necessary?

Sergeant: Necessary? We don't go to the latrine around here without an S47 stroke 19J. Sorry.

At GTSI, we're same way about Microsoft Outlook calendaring. To borrow the phrase, "we don't go to the latrine around here" without an Outlook meeting maker.

(By the way, to answer a question that has haunted me for years, there really never was an "Adam's Ribs."[36] The show's producers made it up. There was briefly a restaurant in the area that changed its name to garner business from the name, but it is long gone, too.)

All kidding and references to TV shows aside, this is where

---

36 Douglas J. Gladstone. "In search of Adam's Ribs - 'Mash' fans keep looking for the Chicago restaurant Hawkeye called from Korea, and guess what they find?". Chicago Sun-Times. April 19, 2009.

you and your business leaders need to carefully evaluate your requirements. In GTSI's case, Google Apps might be a cheaper alternative, but culturally, there was no way we would switch from Outlook. We could continue to host our own Exchange servers. We could use another SaaS provider that interfaces with Microsoft Exchange (like HyperOffice™). We could look at a SaaS provider of Microsoft Exchange®. Or, we could look at Microsoft and their Saas offering Office 365™. Which would be best? That depends on the other requirements, the SLAs and the price. Only by carefully considering and agreeing with the business leaders on the requirements for that service or application can you expect to properly evaluate which options (Cloud among them) are the best for you.

What if I don't consider Cloud?

There is a story that I often tell my customers. One particular customer really embraced server virtualization, so much so that they had clusters in their production data center and in their DR/COOP site several miles away. Their storage was replicating between the two sites. They even had a separate test and development cluster. One day, I asked them, "How do your users request virtual machines or services from you?" He proudly told me that he had developed a form for that very purpose and they promised their users that, once the form was approved, they would have a new virtual machine/service created for them within 5 days. I talked to that customer about overlaying the self-service portal, user interface and chargeback modules (available from VMware, CA, BMC, HP or a host of others) on top of their current infrastructure so that their users could (within certain permissions) request these and have almost immediate access to their needed resources.

Not surprisingly, they didn't budge. Yet three months later, one of their developers called me and said that they had been using a public IaaS Cloud provider for development because it was so easy, fast, and inexpensive. He then informed me they were now ready to launch their application. The full launch would take them over their approved credit card purchasing power every month, so they wanted to purchase it from us at GTSI.

The moral of the story here is self-evident. Users want flexibility in their environments. Users are finding – and will continue to find – ways to "go around" the IT department to accomplish what they need to accomplish. This is happening in agencies and organizations around the country. It's just too easy to give the Cloud provider a credit card and be up and running in 10 minutes.

Are there still applications and data I would not put into a public Cloud? Absolutely. But with Amazon announcing the GovCloud offering (which has FISMA moderate as well as a whole host of other certifications above and beyond their normal environment), we are going to quickly get to a point where less and less data needs to be considered too sensitive for a Public Cloud.
Gus Hunt, the CTO for the Office of the CIO for CIA, said in the Information Week Government article cited below, "your data may be more secure in a public Cloud than behind your firewalls." [37]

How do I procure Cloud?

While procuring something where the bill has a big tendency to change every month based on usage has typically been a problem in the public sector, many government contractors, including GTSI, have taken several public Cloud providers and put them on contract vehicles so you can purchase via not-to-exceed (NTE) purchase orders. Your usage is monitored every month to ensure you do not exceed your NTE amount. We take care of the billing for you and even have the contract vehicles in place. So now, there IS an easy way to procure Public Cloud! And if you want a Private or Hybrid IaaS, or any other Cloud, GTSI would be happy to help you design and architect your Cloud, assist you in designing services, and help you migrate existing applications!

---

37 http://www.informationweek.com/news/government/Cloud-saas/231901640

Remember, Cloud is just one more tool

You've learned about the types of Cloud that are available to you. You have also learned that you are not the first; that public sector people are already using Cloud to save money and deliver better services to their customers. You've learned about the benefits of Cloud and how Cloud might be appropriate for your applications. And now you've learned how to procure Cloud services easily. The only thing left for you to do is to get your head in the Cloud! Find places within your agency where Cloud meets your criteria and use it in the face of the upcoming budget cuts to continue to "do more with less". If you want to know more on Cloud, you can follow my blog at www.gtsiblog.com and I am available on twitter at @GTSI_CTO.

Thanks for reading.

TechAmerica Cloud2 Commission Report

FOREWORD

Cloud technologies are transforming the way computing power is bought, sold and delivered. Rather than purchasing licenses or hardware, users may now obtain computing power as a service, buying only as much as they need, and only when they need it. This new business model brings vast efficiency and cost advantages to government agencies, individuals, and companies of all sizes. The numerous benefits of Cloud computing have already won over many adopters and are generating significant cost savings, efficiencies, flexibility, innovation, and new market opportunities.

This report reflects the growing imperative to fully embrace and capitalize upon the power of Cloud computing. The Commission on the Leadership Opportunity in U.S. Deployment of the Cloud (Cloud2) developed the report at the encouragement of the Federal Chief Information Officer and the U.S. Department of Commerce. The Commission's mandate was to generate recommendations for accelerating adoption of Cloud technologies in the U.S. government and in the commercial space and to identify public policies that will help foster U.S. innovation and leadership in Cloud computing.

The Commission was composed of representatives from 71 companies and organizations, including Cloud providers, Cloud users, and other businesses that are involved in enabling Cloud deployment. To build on this diverse set of expertise and perspectives, the Commissioners interviewed numerous government representatives, heard presentations from a variety of organizations, and analyzed relevant past reports.

Actionable Recommendations — Trust, Transnational Data Flows, Transparency and Transformation

Moving to Cloud computing is a change that involves people, policies, processes, and technology. The Commission identified barriers that have kept some government agencies from moving to the Cloud and recommended actionable solutions to overcome these. In addition, the Commission identified barriers to commercial deployment of Cloud services and recommended actions to eliminate them. Since government, industry and academia share the responsibility to accelerate adoption and drive U.S. innovation and leadership, the recommendations reflect actions for all three key stakeholders. Industry, as represented by the Commission members, is committed to enabling the transition to the Cloud by companies and government agencies and accepts the responsibility for taking actions that enable Cloud adoption.

In this report, the Commission has focused on 14 specific recommendations, categorized into four thematic areas: Trust, Transnational Data Flows, Transparency, and Transformation. For each recommendation, the report identifies why the action is needed, how it should be implemented, who should implement it, and what benefits should be expected from implementation. The Commission intentionally made these recommendations direct and prescriptive.

The four areas are briefly discussed below.

Trust

Users of Cloud computing want assurance that when using Cloud services, their workloads and data will be treated with the highest integrity and their security, privacy, and availability needs will be met. To enable trust and confidence in Cloud services, the Commission recommends that government and industry develop common frameworks, best practices and metrics around security and information assurance to assist users in choosing and deploying the security level most appropriate for their workloads. The Commission also recommends strengthening the identity management ecosystem and data breach laws, as well as supporting increased research on Cloud computing as an investment in future Cloud innovation.

Transnational Data Flows

In a global economy, it is common for businesses to operate in multiple countries and for Cloud providers and users to work and transfer information across national borders. This adds complexity to Cloud adoption because of the data, processes, and people residing on multiple continents with different laws and cultures. In this context, the Commission recommends that industry and the U.S. government promote privacy frameworks, that the U.S. government identify and implement mechanisms to clarify processes and mechanisms around lawful government access to data, and that the U.S. continue international discussions in these areas. We also recommend that the U.S. government lead by example by demonstrating its willingness to trust Cloud computing environments in other countries for appropriate government workloads.

Transparency

Users want an abundance of information about the Cloud services they buy and unfettered access to the data and processes they entrust to the service provider. To meet these needs, Cloud providers must be open and transparent regarding the characteristics and operations of the services they provide. Government and industry should collaboratively develop metrics that facilitate this information sharing and customers' ability to compare Cloud offerings. Additionally, to ensure that data is available to customers should they wish to change Cloud services, Cloud providers should enable porta-bility through industry standards and best practices.

Transformation

The transition to Cloud computing is placing new require-ments on purchasing processes, infrastructure, and people's skills. For government agencies, the fact that buying Cloud computing services can be fundamentally different from buying in-house IT systems poses a challenge. Therefore, agencies, the Office of Management and Budget (OMB), and Congress must demonstrate more flexibility around budget-ing and acquisition processes. Such flexibility, in combination with OMB incentives for moving to the Cloud, will increase the rate of adoption by government agencies. Additionally, to accommodate the bandwidth and reliable connectivity necessary for the growth of Cloud computing, the nation's currently stretched and aging IT broadband infrastructure should be updated, in conjunction with embracing IPv6. To help acquisition and IT personnel understand and carry out the transition to Cloud, government agencies, companies, and academia should develop and disseminate appropriate educational resources.

In addition to the recommendations in the body of the report, the Commission also produced a Cloud Buyer's Guide. The guide walks potential government buyers through questions to ask and steps to take prior to purchasing a Cloud computing solution. Designed to be a living document, the guide is available online at http://www.Cloudbuyersguide.org/. As Cloud technology evolves, this online resource can be easily updated with new frequently asked questions (FAQs) and guidance.

By providing clear, actionable recommendations, the Commission hopes to help accelerate the deployment of Cloud computing at companies and government agencies. Cloud's widespread adoption will drive increased efficiencies and job growth and continue to position the United States as a technology leader in a global marketplace.

Introduction/Purpose of Report

For more than 50 years, the United States has taken advantage of new developments in Information Technology (IT). U.S. companies and government agencies were early adopters of the mainframe computer, the minicomputer, the personal computer, and the World Wide Web. We are now entering a new phase in the history of computing that will be at least as transformative as the mainframe or the Web and provide at least as much benefit to all Americans. Cloud computing represents a powerful new way to provide computing power and storage—and it will unleash huge new opportunities for companies and citizens able to harness it.

Cloud computing is based on a simple idea.[38] By allowing computer users to tap into servers and storage systems scattered

---

38 The National Institute of Standards and Technology, in consultation with industry and government, has drafted a definition of Cloud, including descriptions of the essential characteristics, service models, and deployment models. See http://csrc.nist.gov/publications/drafts/800-145/Draft-SP-800-145_Cloud-definition.pdf.

around the country and around the world—and tied together by the Internet—Cloud service providers can give users better, more reliable, more affordable, and more flexible access to the IT infrastructure they need to run their businesses, organize their personal lives, or obtain services ranging from entertainment to education, e-government, and healthcare. Most Americans already use Cloud computing in one form or another to do email or back up the files on their laptop or smartphone. Most social networking sites and thousands of e-commerce sites (large and small) are running in the Cloud. Cloud computing is not a technology of the future; it is already being used for business and government applications worldwide.

On the other hand, Cloud computing does represent a fundamental shift in how computing is accomplished. The Cloud is not only a new way to more easily and cheaply get the computing power needed to do what companies and individuals are doing today; the Cloud, like the Web, will also generate new business models and drive companies to reorganize and change the way they go to market, team with partners, and serve their customers. It will enable companies (and governments) to move faster and be more responsive and flexible.

Companies will be able to try several prototypes at once, test their limits, and then build and deploy new, better prototypes—all within a few weeks. This may be the most important benefit of the Cloud—it enables companies of all sizes and in all sectors, as well as governments, non-profits, and individuals, to more quickly build new applications and services by reducing the cost and complexity of deploying and managing IT resources. However, that requires Cloud providers to make services simple and easy to use and deploy, and it requires that Cloud customers make the effort to understand the new capabilities Clouds can provide. Most companies and organizations spend the vast majority of their IT budget just maintaining their current infrastructures and the applications that run on them. The Cloud will enable them to devote more resources and talent to creating new products and services and improving productivity.

This democratization of innovation is a huge opportunity for people, organizations, and countries around the world. To maintain its competitive position, the United States must focus on quickly and effectively harnessing the full power of Cloud computing, leading in both the deployment of Cloud and the development of new Cloud services. This will help American companies generate high-paying jobs and compete in the global marketplace.

Whether the United States will benefit as much from this new phase in the evolution of computing as it did from the mainframe and the Web depends upon many factors. Will the iconic U.S. companies that have pioneered and promoted the Cloud continue to lead in the development of Cloud services? Will companies embrace Cloud computing and take advantage of the capabilities it provides? Will the public sector be able to move to the Cloud? Will individuals be comfortable with their data and software located in the Cloud rather than on a device in their hand? Will government policies — both in the United States and abroad — facilitate deployment of and innovation in Cloud services? We firmly believe that the answer to all these questions can and should be an unequivocal YES.

We are convinced that Cloud computing is developing extremely rapidly, much like the Web did in the 1990s, and will have a major impact on computing and the economy. How Cloud computing develops will be shaped by key choices and policy decisions that will be made over the next two or three years. It is critical that industry and government work together to make the right choices.

In some cases, the U.S. government may choose NOT to take action and allow market forces to guide the evolution of the digital economy. U.S. national policies that conflict with those of other countries, even if designed to achieve worthy goals like security or consumer protection, could end up constraining how the Cloud develops or discouraging investment in new Cloud services and applications.

The most effective way for governments to shape the evolution of the Cloud is not through law and regulation but by being smart users of the technology. This is particularly true in the area of security, where some government agencies have especially challenging requirements. As agencies work with industry to ensure that the Cloud services deployed are at least as secure and trusted as the IT systems in use today, the agencies can provide a model that Cloud customers in governments and corporations around the world can emulate.

This report provides recommendations for government, including the White House and key Federal agencies, on how they, in cooperation with industry, academia, and other nations, can (1) adopt policies that will foster development and growth of the Cloud and (2) deploy the Cloud effectively, making government work better, cheaper, and smarter. These recommendations cover a lot of territory but focus on four areas: Trust, Transnational Data Flows, Transparency, and Transformation. Responsibility for success also lies with Cloud providers, and the Commission makes specific recommendations to providers throughout the report. The report also includes a "Buyer's Guide" that advises Federal agencies on how to accelerate adoption of Cloud services.

B

TechAmerica Cloud2SLG Report

Executive Summary and Foreword

Just as political, social and economic structures change and transform society, Information and Communication Technology (ICT) has rapidly evolved to better address consumer and organizational needs. ICT's most recent redefinition has taken shape faster than ever because technology innovation cycles are shrinking. Toward the end of the last decade, a substantial innovation cycle began with three major simultaneous paradigm shifts: widespread use of social media, ubiquitous mobility and pervasive big data.

Now add a fourth sweeping trend to the disruptive technology mix: Cloud computing.

Global IT mega trends for mega business benefits

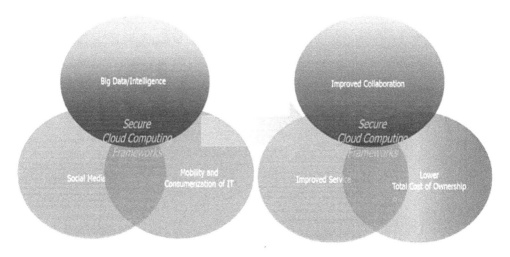

While some initially saw the Cloud excitement as mere hyperbole, those who've used Cloud to solve real-world problems have proven otherwise. Many organizations are realizing important benefits through improved service driven by improved collaboration and integration—all while enjoying the benefit of lower cost. Through shared platforms capable of delivering ICT applications and services, state and local government organizations can do the same.

The timing is fortuitous. Political, social and economic realities are driving federal, state and local governments both to improve services and to save money. Cloud can do both.

Sensing the convergence of these business and technology trends, in September 2011 the TechAmerica Foundation formed a group of experts to develop guidance for helping state and local governments evaluate, adopt and implement Cloud computing. This State and Local Government Cloud Computing (SLG-CC) Commission initiative follows the Foundation's earlier release of a blueprint for the US federal government's adoption of Cloud computing, which supported the Obama Administration's Cloud-first strategy for government technology and for driving U.S. commercial leadership and innovation.

Tarkan Maner, President and CEO of Wyse Technology, leads the Commission. David L. Cohn, Ph.D., Program Director, Smarter Cloud, T.J. Watson Research Center, IBM; and Cisco's Public Sector CTO, Daniel Kent, co-chair the Commission. Numerous experts drawn from business, government and industry serve as SLG-CC commissioners and deputy commissioners (A list of Commissioners and Deputy Commissioners is available at the back of this report and on the Commission's website: SLG-CC Community Portal).

This paper is a distillation of the SLG-CC Commission's efforts. It addresses Cloud access and deployment challenges that are unique to states and localities – including procurement practices – and provides recommendations for surmounting barriers. In producing its recommendations, the Commission considered delivery of critical services to the public, such as healthcare, human services, and education, and discussed ways that large, complex programs can best leverage the Cloud.

While the paper addresses technical subjects, it also covers business and policy issues for a broad audience. A document targeting only technologists would do little to move the adoption of Cloud computing forward or speed the delivery of enhanced government services to constituents. Building on its knowledge of technology innovation and business process re-engineering, the Commission seeks to establish a widely shared communication process that draws all state and local stakeholders into a common Cloud computing vision: better collaboration within and between government agencies; better service to government employees, to the public and to citizens; and all delivered at a better cost to taxpayers.

This paper and the related web portal will not answer all of the questions or address all of issues around Cloud computing for state and local governments. Rather, they will create a knowledge framework for Cloud computing. From the start, the Commission has collaborated with leading state and local government policy makers, ICT executives and vendors to build a basis for further collaboration and idea exchange. The Commission believes Cloud computing and its surrounding technologies will continue to evolve rapidly. As needs and requirements change, technologies and processes will respond. The Commission is dedicated to further develop this paper and the web platform for future needs.

A final thought: This report and its companion web platform are called: "The Cloud Imperative: Better Collaboration, Better Service and Better Cost." The Commission encourages state and local governments to engage on Cloud and, quite frankly, to join the Cloud revolution. While not the last word on this important subject, this white paper does mark the start of an on-going public/private dialogue, describing the business impact of Cloud computing, providing best practices and allowing government employees to leverage what others have done.

So welcome to the Cloud...and to the transformation of ICT-based services in state and local government.

Tarkan Maner, President, CEO and Chief Customer Advocate, Wyse Technology, Inc.

David L. Cohn, Ph.D., Program Director, Smarter Cloud, T.J. Watson Research Center, IBM

Dan Kent, Director Public Sector Solutions & Federal CTO, Cisco Systems, Inc.

Jennifer Kerber, President, TechAmerica Foundation

GTSI Cloud Maturity Model

Step 1 Consolidation	Step 2 Virtualization	Step 3 Automation	Step 4 Utility	Step 5 Cloud
Consolidation & Modernization of Resources	Abstraction & Resource Pooling	Adaptive, Secure, & Repeatable	Self-Service & Metering	On-Demand & Scalable
Server Consolidation	Server & Storage Virtualization	Policy-Based Provisioning & Management	Service Metrics & Metering	IaaS, SaaS, PaaS
Tiered Storage Consolidation	Desktop Virtualization	ITIL-Based Repeatable Processes	Service Level Agreements (SLAs)	Service-Oriented Architecture
Consolidation of Network Services	Virtualized Network Services	Multi-Tier Security	Incident Response & Audit	Inter-Cloud Federation
Consolidation of Disparate Applications	Application Virtualization	Multi-Tier Data Recovery	Continuous Availability & Failover	Integration of Web 2.0 & Web Portals
Key Enabling Capabilities				
Consolidation	Virtualization	ITIL Service Management	DR & COOP	Cloud Internetworking
Modernization	Thin Client Computing	Network Security	Risk / Vulnerability Management	Integration
Power & Cooling	Green IT	Data Center Security	Situational Awareness	Provisioning
High Performance Computing	Data Duplication	Infrastructure Protection	Computing	

Index

A

Amazon XII, 5, 6, 8, 20, 21, 22, 23, 24, 25, 26, 27, 29, 37, 38, 39, 40, 41, 42, 43, 44, 45, 46, 47, 48, 49, 50, 51, 52, 53, 54, 55, 56, 57, 59, 70, 71, 79, 130, 162, 163, 174, 219, 224, 225, 232, 234, 242
Amazon Web Services XII, 6, 8, 20, 21, 23, 40, 41, 42, 43, 44, 45, 46, 48, 49, 50, 51, 52, 53, 54, 55, 56, 57, 59, 219, 225, 234
Anil 209, 210, 211, 212, 214, 217, 218, 234
Anil Karmel 209, 234
App Engine XIII, 7, 127, 128, 129, 130, 132, 133, 134, 135, 137, 139, 140, 142, 143, 144, 145, 147, 148, 152, 157, 163, 234, 235, 239
AppLogic XIV, 186, 190, 204, 205, 206, 207
Arabic 222, 223, 224, 227, 228, 229, 235
ATHLETE 60, 62
AWS XII, 6, 20, 21, 22, 23, 24, 25, 26, 27, 28, 29, 30, 31, 34, 37, 38, 39, 40, 41, 42, 45, 47, 48, 49, 55, 59, 60, 62, 63, 64, 71, 148, 163, 219, 220, 221, 222, 224, 226, 234, 235

B

Barre 149, 150, 151, 153
Belcher, Benton 169

C

CA XIV, 179, 182, 188, 190, 196, 201, 204, 205, 206, 241
Callison-Burch, Chris 224
Catapault 95
CEO IV, V, 1, 254, 255
Cloud2 Commission IV, 244
CloudFront 25
CloudWatch XII, 27, 28, 34, 51, 52, 53, 55, 57
Community Cloud 7, 190, 234
CRM 14, 75, 76, 84, 85, 87, 124, 126, 131, 236, 238

D

Department of Labor 111, 112, 113, 114, 115, 116, 118, 120, 121
DynamoDB 26

E

EC2 XII, 21, 22, 23, 24, 26, 27, 28, 38, 39, 41, 42, 43, 48, 50, 51, 53, 54, 55, 56, 130
Elastic Load Balancer 27

F

Fault Tolerance 177
Fawcett 144
FISMA VII, 23, 29, 69, 121, 238, 242
Fusion CRM 124, 126
Fusion HCM 124, 126

G

Google XIII, 5, 7, 70, 76, 77, 78, 122, 127, 128, 129, 130, 132, 133, 134, 135, 137, 138, 139, 140, 142, 143, 144, 145, 147, 148, 149, 151, 152, 156, 157, 161, 163, 234, 235, 238, 239, 241
Google App Engine XIII, 7, 127, 128, 129, 130, 132, 133, 134, 135, 137, 139, 142, 143, 144, 145, 147, 148, 152, 157, 163, 234, 235, 239
GSA 29, 67, 68, 69, 70, 71, 72
GTSI III, IV, V, XIV, 1, 5, 177, 178, 181, 192, 194, 195, 234, 236, 237, 240, 241, 242, 243, 256

H

HIPAA 23, 67
hybrid Cloud 14, 124, 182
Hybrid Clouds 9, 172, 173, 188, 189, 190, 209, 234, 235
Hyperoffice XIII, 75, 88, 89, 190

I

IaaS XIV, 6, 9, 13, 16, 17, 18, 19, 20, 21, 27, 29, 30, 34, 35, 37, 38, 39, 41, 58, 66, 68, 74, 76, 79, 88, 89, 148, 152, 156, 172, 173, 174, 175, 178, 181, 188, 189, 234, 235, 238, 239, 241, 242, 256
Infrastructure as a Service Cloud. *See also* IaaS
ISC 168, 169

J

Java XIII, 76, 122, 125, 126, 127, 136, 137, 138, 139, 142, 159
Jet Propulsion Laboratory 58
John Hopkins University 222, 224, 227
JPL 58, 59, 60, 61, 62, 63, 64, 65

K

Karmel, Anil 209
Kundra IV, 1, 69, 236

L

LANL XIV, 209, 210, 211, 212, 213, 214, 215, 217, 234
Load Balancers XII, 36, 53, 54, 56, 182
Los Alamos National Labs. *See also* IaaS; *See also* LANL
Lucas 111, 116, 120

M

Massachusetts 149, 150, 151, 154, 156
Mechanical Turk 219, 220, 221, 222, 224, 225, 226, 228, 229, 230, 232, 235
Miami XIV, 32, 165, 166, 167, 168, 169, 170, 171
Microsoft 5, 7, 60, 61, 76, 77, 82, 83, 84, 85, 87, 90, 91, 92, 93, 95, 96, 97, 110, 122, 123, 131, 132, 158, 159, 161, 168, 169, 170, 171, 180, 211, 214, 234, 235, 238, 239, 240, 241
Microsoft Office 365 82, 83, 90, 95, 96
Microsoft Windows Azure 7, 61, 122, 131, 132, 158, 169, 170, 239
Minnesota 90, 91, 92, 95, 96, 97

N

NASA 58, 59, 60, 62, 69
New Zealand 143, 144
NIST XII, 6, 7, 8, 9, 69, 71

O

OET 91, 92, 93, 94, 95, 96, 97
ORACLE 115, 124
Oracle Social Network 124
Osteen 166, 168, 170, 171

P

PaaS V, XIII, 7, 16, 18, 21, 122, 123, 124, 125, 129, 131, 132, 143, 149, 156, 157, 165, 172, 234, 235, 239, 256
Parnell, Carolyn 95
Platform as a Service Cloud 7
Platform as a Service Clouds. *See also* Platform as a Service Cloud
private Cloud 9, 13, 14, 126, 173, 182, 205, 213
Private Cloud. *See also* Private Clouds
Private Clouds 172, 173, 188, 234

R

Rackspace XII, 8, 20, 34, 35, 36, 37, 79

S

SaaS XII, XIII, 6, 9, 14, 18, 73, 74, 75, 76, 77, 78, 79, 80, 82, 83, 84, 85, 88, 90, 92, 93, 99, 110, 111, 112, 113, 114, 118, 121, 123, 124, 133, 162, 163, 172, 189, 190, 234, 235, 236, 238, 239, 240, 241, 256
Salesforce.com XIII, 5, 75, 103, 234, 238
Sarbanes-Oxley 23
Schoolconferences.com XIII, 143, 146
SDK 136, 159, 162, 163
Smith 150, 151
Soderstrom 60, 62, 64
Software as a Service Cloud. *See also* Software as a Service Clouds
Software as a Service Clouds 73
Sonian XII, XIII, 78, 79, 80, 81, 82, 83, 189, 234, 235, 238

T

Taylor 113, 115, 118, 120, 121
TechAmerica IV, 1, 2, 83, 111, 244, 252, 253, 255
Terremark 6, 20, 30, 31, 32, 33, 34, 37, 38, 66, 67, 68, 69, 70, 71, 173, 174, 188, 189, 211, 214, 216, 217, 234
Thin Provisioning 177
Turkers 226, 228, 231

U

USA.Gov 66

V

Valencia, Ed 92
vCenter Chargeback 179, 180
vCloud XIV, 30, 31, 173, 179, 180, 181, 182,
  188, 189, 190, 191, 192, 194, 195, 209, 211, 213
vCloud Director 179, 180, 182, 213
Virtual Distributed Switch 178
VMware XIV, 5, 30, 31, 37, 68, 70, 124, 173,
  175, 175–CCLIX, 176, 178, 179, 180, 182, 188,
  189, 194, 195, 209, 210, 213, 241

W

Wheel of Security 61, 64

Z

Zaidan 223, 224, 225, 227

www.ingramcontent.com/pod-product-compliance
Lightning Source LLC
Chambersburg PA
CBHW051227050326
40689CB00007B/824